I0839890

SPARK

Spark Publishing Group
2026

MILITANT MIND

THE PSYCHOLOGY OF BUILDING WHAT DOESN'T EXIST

SAM BERMAN

Spark-Publishing Group.

ISBN (Paperback): 979-8-218-88545-8
LCCN: 2025926337

Dedication

To my wife, Kate, whose love rebuilt me and has been the quiet engine behind every step of this journey.

To our incredible children, Nathaniel and Samantha "Jane", whose belief in me has been my driving force. This book was written for both of you.

Without all of you, none of this would have been possible.

And to all who believed, and especially to those who didn't...
may this book stand as a testament to the power of love, resilience, and unwavering strength.

"The life you want demands the death of who you were."

-Unknown

Contents

Prologue

Who I Am, and Why You Should Care

Before you invest your time in the pages ahead, before you decide whether my perspective is worth listening to, you deserve to know who I am and why I'm writing this book. Not the polished version. Not the curated biography crafted to impress a conference audience. Not the sequence of accomplishments that looks linear in hindsight but was erratic and uncertain while it unfolded. You deserve the honest story behind the person asking for your attention, your curiosity, and perhaps even a small piece of your belief in what you might be capable of becoming.

My name is Sam Berman, and today I'm the Founder and CEO of the Logistics Advanced Research Center (LARC), a company based in Nashville, Tennessee, that designs advanced reusable shipping platforms for the world's most valuable technology: AI servers, semiconductor equipment, aerospace systems, medical equipment and the sensitive hardware that keeps the modern world running. But the role I hold today, the authority implied by the title, wasn't inherited or prewritten. It wasn't born from privilege or predictability. It was built through years of fragmentation, rebuilding, and relentless drive. Before LARC existed, I'd already started several other companies, each one shaped by intuition and necessity more than opportunity. None of it came easily, but each venture taught me something essential about who I was becoming and what I was capable of creating.

I wasn't raised with entrepreneurial frameworks or early advantages. I wasn't the kid who ran childhood businesses or devoured books on wealth creation. My early life was shaped far more by instability and emotional chaos than by mentorship or resources. I learned to survive long before I learned to aspire. My life should've conditioned me to stay small, to fear risk, to cling to whatever security I could find. And yet, even in those early years, something in me resisted. A persistent sense that the life around me didn't match the magnitude of what I felt stirring inside. I couldn't name it, but I could feel it, the unmistakable pressure of a future that refused to let me settle.

The true turning point in my life wasn't a moment of inspiration but a collapse. A long, painful unraveling that scattered every part of my identity. Emotionally, financially, spiritually, I fell through the floor I thought I was standing on.

I found myself alone with almost nothing to my name and no clear sense of how to rebuild. It was the kind of season that forces you to meet yourself honestly, stripped of distraction. And in that emptiness, something unexpected began to form. I didn't know it then, but the collapse wasn't the end. It was the clearing. It was the demolition required before reconstruction.

What remained, when everything else was gone, was the instinct to rebuild, not just my life, but myself. A small ember of belief that refused to die. And it was from that ember, which turned to a roaring fire, that LARC was ultimately born. Not in a boardroom, not in an incubator, and not in the hands of consultants or investors. LARC began as a crude drawing on the back of a napkin in a restaurant, a sketch of a better way to move the world's most valuable technology, born from frustration, insight, and the stubborn conviction that the future deserved something far better than disposable wooden crates. From that napkin sketch came prototypes. From prototypes came failures and revisions. And from revisions came momentum. Today, that sketch has evolved into a global platform used by some of the largest and most influential companies in the world, proof that the smallest ideas, when rooted in purpose and perseverance, can reshape entire industries.

I share this not to create mystique or inflate my story, but to give context for the pages that follow. This book won't teach you how to pitch investors or structure a cap table. It won't tell you how to run ads or optimize your operations. There are plenty of books for those things. This one is about everything those books leave out, the psychological war, the identity rupture, the moments of collapse, the rebuilding of the self, and the relentless inner work required to build anything meaningful. This is a book about the internal architecture of entrepreneurship, the part no one talks about because it's messy, ugly, painful, disorienting, and deeply personal.

This journey is about obsession, the force that anchors you before you even understand what it's pulling you toward. It's about doubt, the quiet antagonist that must be outgrown if you want to build anything that lasts. It's about resilience, the part of you made in darkness, in betrayal, in loss, in the moments no one will ever see. It's about the moment you refuse to keep living small, the moment the fracture inside you becomes too powerful to suppress, the moment you begin to move toward a life that demands courage. And it's about the scar tissue that becomes your greatest competitive advantage.

Above all, this book rests on a single truth: entrepreneurship doesn't begin with an idea. It begins with identity. It begins long before the world sees anything, in the moments when you confront who you are and who you refuse to remain.

This book is my story, but only as a vehicle, because the truth is, at some level, it's every builder's story. The details are mine. The psychology belongs to all of us. I don't do this to solicit admiration or sympathy, but to show you that every chapter ahead was earned in seasons of collapse, in nights of doubt, in moments when I had nothing but the stubborn instinct and deep faith to keep moving. If you've ever felt underestimated, broken, out of place, or haunted by the sense that you're meant for something larger than your circumstances, then this book is yours as much as it's mine.

So let us begin.

Introduction
Building What Doesn't Exist

I never set out to write a book about the psychology of entrepreneurship. For most of my life, I was too busy trying to survive to imagine stopping long enough to capture any of it. Writing felt like something other people had the luxury to do, people whose lives followed cleaner arcs, whose stories fit neatly into the kind of narratives you hear on podcasts or read in business magazines. My path never felt like that. It felt raw, unpredictable, often painful, and shaped by forces that had nothing to do with market timing or strategy. Yet the idea of writing this book arrived anyway, faint and unexpected, at a moment when I wasn't looking for it.

It happened on a day that felt strangely full circle. LARC's cofounder, Chris Taylor, and I were standing at the front of a classroom at Belmont University, guest lecturing for our friend and longtime supporter, Dr. John Gonas. We were speaking to his finance students about raising capital for early stage companies. My relationship with Belmont wasn't deep in the traditional sense. I'd only spoken there a few times, but those appearances mattered. They were meaningful checkpoints in our journey, moments where the university gave us a platform, opened doors, and helped introduce LARC to the broader Nashville community. In fact, it was at Belmont where we officially launched LARC. And standing there always carried a bit of irony for me. I'm a college dropout with no degree in anything, someone who walked away from academia because the structure never fit the way my mind worked. Yet here I was, at the front of a classroom, being asked to teach the very students pursuing the education I never completed.

Chris handled most of the technical discussion that day, explaining capital formation with the kind of clarity and sequence that made the process sound almost orderly. But as I watched the students listening to him, something inside me pushed against the neatness of the narrative. Maybe it was the belief in their eyes that success begins with clean diagrams, pitch decks, and capital strategies. Maybe it was the memory of my own beginnings, which were anything but academic. Or maybe it was the simple truth that the real entrepreneurial journey never starts with money. It starts long before the textbooks, long before the strategies, long before the classroom, in the places no curriculum can reach.

So instead of talking about funding and valuations, I asked a different question, one that was simple but revealing. "How many of you think that the most important part of starting any new venture is actually your relationships?"

The room fell silent. A few students shrugged. A few exchanged uncertain glances. Only one or two hands lifted, and even those hands rose halfheartedly, more out of politeness than conviction. At the back of the room, Dr. Gonas, a man with deep business experience, connections, and understanding of how the system really works, almost violently shook his head yes, the way someone nods when they're trying to will the answer onto others in the room.

In that silence, something crystallized. These students were bright, talented, and ambitious, but they were about to step into a world that academia had prepared them to understand intellectually, not psychologically. They believed entrepreneurship was primarily about ideas, business models, funding rounds, market conditions. They hadn't been taught that the real journey takes place internally. They hadn't been warned that the true battlefield is always the self. They had no sense of how relationships, the people you trust, the alliances and teams you form, the betrayals you endure, can determine the entire trajectory of a life. They knew balance sheets. They had no idea how to recognize emotional manipulation, manage despair, recover from loss, or rebuild themselves after everything collapses.

As I stood there, I realized something startling: nearly everything taught about entrepreneurship is incomplete. Not wrong, just superficial. Sanitized. Stripped of the parts that carry actual consequence. Universities teach the mechanics of business. Podcasts offer the tactics. Business books deliver frameworks and models that fit neatly onto six by nine pages. But no one teaches what happens behind all of that. No one teaches the psychological structure you must build if you want to survive the parts of the journey that aren't photographed or publicized. No one talks about the toll. No one explains the identity you must shed, or the one you must grow into. No one warns you about what it feels like when your past begins to sabotage your future, or when the people you trust turn out to be the ones who set the trapdoor beneath your feet.

Standing in that classroom, looking at those students who still believed the journey would be linear if they worked hard enough, I understood the real reason I was there. I wasn't supposed to give them the PG movie version. I was supposed to tell the truth. Not because I had all the answers, but because I'd lived through the parts no one talks about. The parts founders hide. The parts where you get knocked so low you lose sight of who you are. The parts where your identity gets crushed and you're forced to confront what you've been avoiding for years. The parts that develop whatever strength you eventually become known for.

This book isn't a playbook. It isn't a system or a step by step guide. It isn't a motivational manual dressed in business language. This book is a psychological field guide for the builders, the misfits, the warriors, the ones who can't stop moving toward something bigger even when everything around them is trying to hold them back. It's for the people who feel the breach inside them and know, even if they can't articulate it, that the life they were handed is too small for the person they're becoming. It's for those who understand, or are beginning to understand, that entrepreneurship isn't about starting a company. It's about becoming someone capable of carrying one.

The journey begins where every real entrepreneurial story begins, not with a pitch deck, a business idea, or a spark of inspiration. It begins inside the mind. Inside the discomfort. Inside the quiet, irreversible moment when you realize that there's no turning back. It begins where the fracture first appears. It begins where the fire starts. And it begins with the understanding that everything you build externally will ultimately be a reflection of what you build internally.

This is where the story really begins.

"The wound is the place where light enters you."

-Rumi

1

The Fracture and the Call

Transformation never begins the way people imagine it. It doesn't start with an idea, a moment of inspiration, a mentor, or a business plan. It begins with something quieter, far more internal: a fracture. A subtle break in the composition of the self. A tension so faint at first that it's easy to dismiss. You notice it the way a homeowner notices the first hairline crack in a wall, not with alarm, but with unavoidable awareness. Something has shifted. Something foundational is under stress. Something is beginning to give.

Most people learn to ignore that feeling. They bury it beneath routine, rationality, distraction, obligation, anything that keeps them tethered to what's familiar. They become experts at bargaining with their own discomfort, convincing themselves that unease is simply a phase that will pass. But there's a different kind of person, the kind who eventually builds and leads, who can't silence the fracture once it begins to widen. For them, the break isn't a warning. It's an invitation.

I felt that invitation earlier than I understood it. As a child, classrooms felt too restrictive for the way my mind worked. Not because I resisted learning, I loved learning, but because the structure felt wrong. The world wanted compliance. My mind wanted expansion. That tension created a persistent sense of misalignment, though I couldn't have named it then. I only knew I felt confined by systems that seemed designed for someone else.

But fractures rarely break open in childhood. They accumulate. They hide beneath the surface until something heavy enough presses against them.

When I was sixteen, the first major weight arrived in my life. My father died suddenly at just forty eight years old, and with him went the sense of safety I'd always taken for granted. One day I was imagining the milestones ahead, graduation, freedom, possibility, maybe even a college football career and the next, I was staring into a void that had no shape, no explanation, no familiar edges. There's no guidebook for losing a parent at sixteen. You adapt because you have no choice. You move forward because standing still feels like drowning. You harden because softness feels like exposure.

But even after the world steadies, the fracture caused by that loss remains. It becomes part of your foundation, unseen but structural. You learn to build around it.

Not even a decade later, another weight arrived, slow, brutal, and impossible to outrun. My mother became ill. Her decline reshaped time itself. Days stretched into a haze of hospital rooms, phone calls, and updates that felt like emotional whiplash. Hope rose and fell until hope itself became a fragile thing. Watching her fade was like watching the last familiar pillar of my early life crumble in slow motion.

And in that vulnerable space, where grief had already carved me open, a second fracture appeared. Someone I trusted, someone whose presence should've offered steadiness during that season, instead withdrew. But it was more than absence. Grief reveals what's hollow and what's real, and what emerged wasn't just distance but something that deepened the pain I was already in.

Small absences became patterns. Warmth evaporated. There were moments when my pain was treated as an inconvenience, when vulnerability seemed to irritate rather than move. I didn't recognize it as cruelty then. You don't want to believe that someone you trusted is intentionally causing harm, especially during the worst moments of your life. But slowly, it became clear. The timing wasn't accidental.

Loss collided with this reality in ways that left me disoriented. It didn't just hurt. It dislodged something fundamental. It shook the internal compass I'd relied on, gutted a part of me I didn't know was vulnerable, left me questioning my judgment and my understanding of people. Only later would I learn that what I faced wasn't simply a failing of character, but a severe personality disorder. It was a level of brokenness and darkness I couldn't have fixed or stopped, damage beyond my control or comprehension.

And with that realization came a measure of understanding, though not yet peace. This wound, painful as it was, existed alongside others. The grief of my mother's decline, the fracture of trust, the gradual erosion of what I'd built, these weren't separate battles. They were part of the same unraveling. I didn't know it then, but this convergence, brutal as it felt, would become the catalyst for something I couldn't yet see.

And in the aftermath of all of it, after the last of my mother's strength slipped away, after the relationship collapsed into something unrecognizable, after the emotional terrain underneath me gave out, I found myself standing inside an empty apartment. Not metaphorically empty. Literally. No furniture. No bed. No comfort. Just a bare floor and a silence so complete it pressed against me like a weight on my chest.

There are moments when identity crumbles loudly, and there are moments when it simply dissolves in the dim light of an empty room. This was the latter. A slow dissolution of the self I'd been. A disintegration of the story I'd been living. A realization that I was standing on the rubble of a decade of survival. Lying on that cold floor, I understood something my mind wasn't yet ready to articulate: The version of myself that had brought me this far was gone. The demolition was finished. The clearing had begun. And the fracture, long ignored, long managed, long denied, had finally split wide open. But in that splitting, in that complete breaking apart, something unexpected emerged.

Not hope, not yet. But a strange sense of relief. The weight of pretending was gone. The exhaustion of holding together what was already broken had lifted. I had nothing left to lose because everything had already been lost. And in that stark reality, there was a kind of freedom I'd never known. The floor was solid beneath me. The walls were still standing. I was still breathing. And somewhere, beneath the grief and the pain and the disorientation, I sensed that this moment wasn't the end of my story. It was the prerequisite for what came next. I didn't know how yet. I didn't know when. But I knew, with a quiet certainty that felt almost absurd given the circumstances, that I would find a way through this. Knowing that was enough...but just barely enough.

Collapse

The truth about collapse is that it never arrives with the clarity we imagine from a distance, feeling not like the start of anything but like an ending, a sudden dislocation from the life you thought you were living and the identity you thought you understood. When everything falls apart at once, the human instinct isn't to rebuild, but to simply survive the impact, your breath shortening, your vision narrowing, and your mind becoming small and protective, focused only on making it through the next hour or the next day. For a while, that was all I could do. Lying on the floor of that empty apartment, I felt an exhaustion that sleep couldn't touch. It wasn't physical or emotional, but something far deeper, something that lived under the surface of everything I thought I knew about myself. It was the exhaustion of someone who'd been holding up too much weight for too long, someone who'd endured loss layered upon loss until endurance itself became a burden.

In that space, I wasn't thinking about ambition or future or purpose. I wasn't thinking like an entrepreneur. I was thinking like someone who'd stumbled into the deepest version of himself, stripped, raw, unguarded, and was trying to understand how to climb out of it. Yet collapse, as destructive as it is, has its own kind of intelligence. It removes everything unnecessary. It strips away distractions. It forces honesty. All the narratives you tell yourself to avoid discomfort fall silent, and only the truth remains. And the truth that slowly surfaced for me wasn't the cruelty I'd endured or the grief I was drowning in. Those were visible. What was deeper and more enduring was the fracture inside me that had been widening for years, the fundamental gap between the life I'd built to survive and the life I was meant to create.

Pain doesn't invent new truths; it reveals the ones you've been refusing to acknowledge. In the silence of that room, I realized that I'd spent years negotiating with myself, trying to fit into a version of life that had never suited me. I'd endured, tolerated, adapted, and compromised. I'd shaped myself around what was expected or practical, believing that stability required shrinking.

But what I'd endured in those months made something undeniable: I could no longer return to who I'd been. I'd lost too much, seen too much, felt too much to ever fit back inside the old self.

As those days blurred into weeks, I felt a strange internal shift, a friction that had nothing to do with anxiety and everything to do with honesty. It was as if a quiet part of me, one I'd ignored for years, was finally growing loud enough to confront. I felt an agitation at the idea of going back to anything that resembled the life I'd lived before, not because that life had been unbearable, but because I now understood how small it'd been. When you carry trauma for long enough, you begin to confuse survival with identity. You start believing that endurance is your natural state rather than a temporary response to extraordinary circumstances. I'd built an entire internal world around that belief, and suddenly, it no longer held.

The Call

The Call, whatever that force is that pulls a person into their next self, doesn't arrive like inspiration or motivation. It arrives like pressure. A light but insistent pushing from the inside, a discomfort that becomes progressively harder to ignore. I didn't feel clarity, but I felt the unmistakable sense that remaining who I'd been was now emotionally impossible. Something inside me was demanding expansion. Something inside me was refusing to let collapse be the conclusion. It wasn't ambition. It wasn't excitement. It was a refusal, a refusal to stay broken, a refusal to stay small, a refusal to allow the cruelty of another person to become the defining shape of my future.

As this internal shift continued, I became aware of how much of my identity had been constructed out of necessity rather than choice. I saw how self reliance, once a protective layer, had also become a cage. I saw how endurance had become a form of emotional confinement. I saw how the life I'd pieced together was shaped more by fear and memory than by desire or possibility. Awareness is the first act of rebellion. It disrupts the patterns you've lived inside for years. It reveals how you've been contorting yourself to fit inside a story that was never meant to be yours permanently.

Eventually, I began to see that the emptiness around me wasn't only loss, it was also space. Space that grief had exposed. Space that the collapse had cleared. Space that I'd never possessed in my adult life because I'd been too busy surviving to create anything new. That space scared me at first. It disoriented me. But it also drew me forward. I didn't yet know what I would become, but I could feel that I couldn't remain who I'd been.

The fracture inside me had split wide open. The old identity was losing its grip. The Call had begun, insistent, unavoidable. And beneath all the pain, beneath all the confusion, beneath all the exhaustion, something else began to surface: the early, faint recognition that collapse hadn't destroyed me. It had revealed me. And now, whether I felt ready or not, the process had begun.

As the days and weeks continued to settle around me, something in the internal landscape began to shift in a way I hadn't anticipated. The pain remained, the loss remained, and the echoes of what I'd endured didn't vanish, but they began to take on a different shape. They became less of a wound and more of a doorway. The same memories that had crushed me now pointed toward something beyond the collapse itself. Grief no longer simply felt like an ending; it felt like an initiation. And as I moved through the remnants of that difficult period, I realized that the demolition of my old life had cleared a path I'd never had the courage or clarity to walk before.

There comes a moment after enough has been taken from you, when you've been exhausted, broken open, and stripped down, when survival stops being enough. The instinct to endure, once necessary, becomes a limitation. What once protected you becomes a cage. And in that moment, your relationship to yourself begins to change. You stop clinging to the past so desperately, stop negotiating with your own unhappiness, stop pretending that the life you had is the life you still want. What emerges in that space isn't motivation, but truth. The truth that who you were isn't who you must become. The truth that collapse, as brutal as it is, can also be a form of release. The truth that a life built on survival can't carry you into a life built on creation.

That realization was the beginning of the path forward, not because I felt strong or inspired, but because something inside me refused to let despair write the final chapter. I began to see that the fracture within me, the same fracture that had caused so much internal conflict for years, wasn't a flaw. It was the beginning of identity change. It was the first evidence of growth. It was the part of me that knew I was meant for more and was finally done being ignored. I wasn't ready in any conventional sense. I wasn't clear. I wasn't healed. But I was willing. And willingness, more than confidence or certainty, is what transformation actually requires.

This willingness signaled the end of the survival identity I'd been living inside for so long. The version of me that had carried childhood grief, navigated instability, and withstood emotional violence had served a purpose, but it wasn't equipped to lead me into the next chapter. The instinct to protect rather than expand, to tolerate rather than demand, to endure rather than create, had reached its limit. For the first time in my life, I could feel myself stepping out of that old version of me, not all at once, not with fanfare, but in small, decisive shifts that began to redirect the trajectory of my entire future.

And this is the truth at the center of every entrepreneurial journey: it doesn't begin with an idea but with identity, in the psychological space where the life you've been living becomes incompatible with the person you're meant to become. People imagine entrepreneurship springs from opportunity, inspiration, or talent, but those are surface elements. The real beginning is internal. It's the moment when the fracture becomes impossible to ignore, when the familiar becomes too small to hold you, when the discomfort of staying where you are outweighs the fear of stepping into the unknown.

Entrepreneurs aren't born in moments of confidence, but in moments when confidence doesn't matter. They emerge from internal contradiction from the pull of something greater and the push of something intolerable. They emerge when protecting themselves from the world becomes less important than contributing something to it. They emerge when the cost of inaction becomes unbearable. They emerge when the old identity dics and the new identity is still forming, raw and uncertain, but undeniable.

As I stood inside the ruins of my old life, I began to sense that what I'd endured wasn't an interruption of my story, but the preparation for it. Pain had sharpened my awareness. Loss had stripped me bare. Cruelty had forced me to confront truths I'd avoided. And that empty apartment, the symbol of everything that had fallen apart, slowly became the birthplace of everything that would eventually rise. I didn't yet know that LARC would come. I didn't yet know that I would build companies or shape industries or push myself into spaces I'd once believed were meant for other people. I didn't yet know the scale of what would come next. But I could feel the faint outline of something forming, a vision that didn't yet have details, but had weight, direction, and inevitability.

This book, and this chapter specifically, is meant to guide the reader into that understanding. The journey of becoming an entrepreneur isn't about chasing an idea or following a template. It's about confronting yourself, your pain, your patterns, your limitations, your losses, and using them as the raw material for evolution. It's about developing the emotional resilience required to build something that doesn't exist yet. It's about learning to trust your own instincts even when they pull you away from the stability you once clung to. It's about recognizing that the life you want requires the death of the life you were willing to tolerate.

The goal of this journey isn't simply to help someone start a business. It's to help them build the internal architecture that makes success sustainable. Because without that foundation, without the identity transformation that precedes the external accomplishments, every entrepreneur eventually collapses under the weight of their own unaddressed fractures. The world will challenge you, competition will pressure you, failure will test you, and doubt will whisper to you. Those challenges destroy people who haven't rebuilt themselves from the inside out. But when you've gone through the internal demolition and reconstruction required to answer your own Call, those challenges don't break you. They refine you. They strengthen you. They become the fuel that drives you forward.

That's where this book is leading the reader: toward the understanding that entrepreneurship isn't primarily a matter of strategy but of identity. Toward the recognition that vision without transformation is fragile, but transformation without vision is incomplete. Toward the realization that the fracture isn't the end of something, but the beginning. And toward the ultimate truth that every great builder, every great founder, every great creator begins not with a brilliant idea, but with one defining moment, the moment they finally decide that the life they've been living is no longer big enough for the person they're meant to be.

"I am not talented. I'm Obsessed"

-Conor McGregor

2

Obsession: The Fuel No One Talks About

Obsession doesn't announce itself. It arrives as friction, a low-grade discomfort that accumulates so gradually you can pretend it isn't there, yet persists with enough force that you never get a moment's peace from it. Before it becomes the engine driving everything you make, before it transforms into the merciless momentum that pulls you through catastrophe and reinvention, it manifests as restlessness, as dissatisfaction, as the gnawing conviction that you're fundamentally out of step with everyone around you, that the life others inhabited without question felt constricting, mechanical, too predetermined for whatever wiring ran through me.

I learned young that the world runs on predictable rails and makes you pay for jumping off. School delivered that lesson first, not because I couldn't do the work but because I refused to fold myself into the rigid channels classrooms required. Where teachers identified problems, I tracked patterns. What they treated as gospel, I questioned. The answers I wanted, they had no interest in providing. Childhood obsession doesn't arrive wrapped as a gift, it shows up as conflict, as friction, as being labeled "difficult," "stubborn," "unfocused," "defiant," when you're just built to process reality differently than the standardized machinery was designed to accommodate.

My father, a Vietnam veteran out of Brooklyn, was withdrawn, carried his wars inside him, and had no blueprint for redirecting the intensity in me. He valued order, stability, structure. In our house, respect mattered. Work ethic mattered. But we didn't speak in emotional vocabulary. What existed between us was proximity more than closeness, the kind of careful distance that settles between fathers and sons who never learned each other's language. My mother, raised in a small West Virginia town, ran on a different frequency entirely. Warm, intuitive, fiercely loving, she held an unshakeable belief that I possessed capabilities the world hadn't recognized yet. She understood the current moving through me before either of us had words for it, and she guarded it in ways I wouldn't fully comprehend until years had passed.

But obsession ignores the safety of your foundation or the affection surrounding you. It drags you relentlessly away from anything resembling ordinary. Even young, even as a teenager, I understood my life wouldn't follow conventional architecture, a realization that landed not as self-assurance, but as pure, restless agitation.

A low hum in my chest insisted I was meant to build something, challenge something, bring into existence what didn't yet exist. I couldn't articulate it then. I only knew that ordinary bored me and predictable irritated me.

The full force of obsession revealed itself in the years that followed, years carved out by loss, instability, and a violent acceleration into adulthood. I won't retrace the ground already covered in Chapter One; those contours are already embedded in the narrative. What matters here is what those experiences ignited. When everything you've built your life on gets stripped away, when the ground beneath you collapses entirely, only two outcomes exist: you break, or something inside you crystallizes into a different form. For me, what came was obsession. Pure, unfiltered, all-consuming obsession. Not with success, but with building. With forward motion. With refusing to let circumstances, even catastrophic ones, determine where I was headed.

Obsession became my internal scaffolding when every external structure had failed. It wasn't noble. It wasn't romantic. It probably wasn't even healthy. It was survival. A psychological mechanism hammered into existence out of necessity. Where others sought comfort or escape, I found myself pulled repeatedly toward creation, toward ideas, toward the compulsion to solve problems most people weren't even considering. Obsession isn't about enjoying something. It's about being incapable of setting it down. Unable to release it. Unable to quiet the drive long enough to pretend you want anything approximating a normal life.

By the time I landed in Silicon Valley in my mid-twenties, I understood obsession enough to recognize it separated me from most people in my orbit. Fifteen years in that ecosystem confirmed that innovation doesn't emerge from the balanced, the moderate, or the comfortable. It emerges from those who cannot stop. Those who lie awake turning problems over in their minds. Those who feel fundamentally incomplete until they've built something. Those who can't explain why the compulsion exists, only that they'd suffocate without it.

In that world, I stopped pretending this intensity was something I could switch off. Silicon Valley didn't reward people who dabbled, it exposed them. What it demanded, what it required, was a particular kind of internal combustion that never fully powers down. I began recognizing that what others diagnosed as imbalance was actually the essential fuel for creation. The deeper I leaned into it, the more clearly everything around me came into focus.

It was during those years that I began understanding obsession wasn't just some personality trait. It was the operating system running beneath everything I built. It was why I'd started multiple companies long before LARC. It was why I could spot inefficiencies others walked right past and felt compelled to fix them. And it was why I struggled to stay inside any structure I hadn't created myself.

But obsession doesn't just build companies. It builds moments, crossroads that reshape your entire trajectory. One of those moments arrived during what should have been an unremarkable lunch with a guy who ran a wood crating company. He mentioned casually that he was crating hundreds of server racks, describing a process that struck me as wasteful, slow, expensive, stuck in the past. Wood and screws and a system that hadn't changed in centuries. I joked about wrapping the racks in a giant cardboard tube. He laughed. Got up to use the bathroom. And in those five minutes, obsession hijacked everything.

When he came back, I wasn't eating. I was sketching. Not deliberately, not strategically, but compulsively, lines and angles and modular walls scrawled across a napkin. That moment would become the origin of LARC, though neither of us knew it then. But that's how obsession works: it converts throwaway moments into turning points. It sees past what exists and insists the impossible be dragged into reality. That napkin sketch wasn't genius. It was inevitability. Obsession had been driving toward it for years. And it was only the start.

The Misfit's Furnace

Obsession doesn't grow in the bright, polished moments of life. It grows in friction, those early collisions between who you are and who the world insists you should be. For some people, childhood is where they learn to adapt. For me, it was where I learned I couldn't. I didn't have the wiring for complacency or the patience for routines designed to flatten the mind into submission. I had a restless, accelerated curiosity that refused to sit still. I had anger I couldn't name, intensity I couldn't dilute, and a refusal to accept the invisible rules everyone else seemed willing to live by.

People like imagining that entrepreneurs are born with some kind of early clarity, lemonade stands, childhood hustles, mini empires run from bedrooms. That wasn't my story. If anything, my childhood was defined by misalignment, a persistent sense that the structures I was placed in were far too narrow for the questions flooding my head. Teachers mistook my boredom for inability. The classroom mistook my frustration for defiance.

The system mistook my intensity for something that needed fixing. But obsession has no place in standardized environments. It refuses to be boxed in by worksheets or timelines or the slow drip of curriculum designed to keep kids predictable.

When my third grade teacher wanted to shove me into remedial classes, she wasn't seeing a deficit in ability, she was seeing a deficit in compliance. My mother, whose instincts ran deeper than any test score, pushed back hard. And when the results came in, gifted, highest the examiner had ever recorded nothing changed because the problem had never been aptitude. The world expected me to function on its rhythm when I was already operating at a different frequency entirely.

That tension followed me through adolescence. While my friends coasted through the standard rituals of growing up, I couldn't settle. I felt a constant urge to push against something, to test limits, to find the edges of whatever system contained me. It wasn't rebellion for its own sake. It was instinct—raw, unrefined, disruptive instinct. A sense that the world was packed with broken structures begging to be torn down and rebuilt. If someone told me "this is just how things are," my immediate response was suspicion. Why? Who decided that? Is it true? Is it efficient? Is it rational? Could it be better? This wasn't a recipe for smooth adolescence. But it was the foundation for everything that came later.

Obsessive personalities don't blend in. They collide. With authority. With expectations. With complacency. With systems. With themselves. I was constantly at odds with the world around me, not because I craved conflict, but because I couldn't stomach the numbness of conformity. When people saw anger rising in me, they saw volatility. What they missed was the deeper truth that anger was just energy searching for direction. Fire without a container.

It would take years to understand that obsession isn't born from comfort; it's born in the places where your nature grinds against the world like sandpaper. Every misfit moment, every misunderstanding, every accusation of being "too much" or "too intense" or "too difficult" is actually the furnace where obsession gets shaped. And the hotter the furnace, the sharper the blade.

When my father died during my teens, the furnace intensified. Though we weren't emotionally close, the loss carved out a kind of void, an unexpected silence I couldn't make sense of. The house shifted. The world shifted. My mother held the pieces together as best she could, but the absence of my father, even without emotional closeness, shifted the gravitational pull of my life. It shoved me faster into adulthood, faster into self-reliance, faster into the urgency that would eventually define my entrepreneurial identity. Survival became my operating system before ambition ever showed up.

The second great loss—my mother—did something even deeper. It split the ground beneath everything I trusted. Chapter One already walked through that collapse, and I won't repeat it, but I'll say this: obsession often grows strongest in the wreckage. When everything familiar dissolves, when the world becomes unrecognizable, when grief and betrayal land in the same moment, something inside you either shatters or rewires itself. My rewiring came as an unyielding drive to rebuild, not just my life, but myself. That drive was obsession wearing its real face.

You learn things in the dark you can't learn anywhere else. You learn that motivation is worthless, discipline falls short, passion is too fragile. What carries you through devastation is something harder, something far less appealing: compulsion. The need to create. The need to build. The need to move. Obsession becomes the rope you grip when you're climbing out of a hole. It becomes the oxygen you pull when the air gets thin. It becomes the voice that whispers, even when you're broken, that there's something on the other side of this pain and you won't leave this world until you find it. That kind of fire isn't taught. It's tempered.

By the time I reached Silicon Valley, that fire had shaped me. Fourteen years inside the machinery of logistics and supply chain systems did more than teach me the mechanics of an industry, it exposed the fault lines, the inefficiencies, the absurdities embedded everywhere. While others accepted the system as it was, I couldn't stop pulling it apart, analyzing it, hunting for its weaknesses. Obsession had turned me into a tracker of inefficiency, a predator of stagnation. If there was a better way to do something, I could sense it in my bones long before I could articulate it. That instinct isn't learned. It's forged in the furnace.

But obsession alone isn't enough. It needs direction. It needs context. It needs a problem worthy of its intensity. And the problem found me the day I sat at that lunch meeting with the wood crating company. What started as casual conversation about outdated, expensive wooden boxes split my obsession open like a fault line under pressure. When he mentioned the thousands of dollars being spent per crate, when he described a process that felt like a relic of ancient manufacturing, something clicked. The world was moving forward at breakneck speed, data centers, robotics, semiconductors, aerospace—and yet the very infrastructure moving that technology was stuck in a prehistoric model. Wood. Screws. Waste. Damage. Delay.

The man stepped away from the table, and in the span of minutes, the sketch poured out of me. Not thoughtfully. Not strategically. Instinctively. Obsessively. By the time he came back, the napkin was covered with lines, angles, and modular concepts that would eventually become the foundation of LARC.

This is what people miss about obsession: it doesn't ask for permission. It doesn't wait for preparation. It doesn't need time, or planning, or a committee. When obsession spots a problem, it solves it in real time. It bypasses the rational mind completely. It moves through you like a force of nature. All you can do is try to keep up.

But the napkin sketch wasn't the peak of obsession, it was the ignition point. The moment when the fire finally found its target. The world was still running on wood and wishful thinking, and I saw the opening to build something radically better, something engineered for speed, protection, sustainability, precision. Something that actually made sense for the technology it carried. Something worthy of the future.

Only later would people call it innovation. In the moment, it was simply necessity meeting a really big idea.

Obsessive people aren't driven by choice. They're driven by compulsion. And that compulsion, when paired with the right crack, the right loss, the right glimpse of possibility, is enough to build an empire.

The Edge That Survives

Obsession, once awakened, never really sleeps again. It becomes the silent structure of your decisions, the unspoken rhythm of your days, the invisible force shaping your future long before anyone else can see the outlines forming. People think obsession is loud, manic, all-consuming in obvious ways. And sometimes it is. But the most powerful form of obsession is quiet. It works in the background, beneath every thought, informing every instinct, sharpening every question. It becomes the lens through which you interpret the world.

By the time LARC emerged from that napkin sketch, I understood something about myself with a clarity I'd never possessed before: I wasn't driven by ambition, or success, or recognition, but by an unrelenting internal need to fix what was broken, to build what didn't exist, to attack inefficiency with almost moral intensity. The world saw wooden boxes. I saw an outdated system begging to be rebuilt. People saw an industry too entrenched to change. I saw an opportunity so obvious it felt offensive to ignore.

But obsession isn't just about seeing what others don't see. It's about refusing to look away once you've seen it.

And that refusal isn't romantic. It isn't poetic. It isn't the kind of passion that fits neatly into a commencement speech. It's more like an ache, a vibration, a near physical discomfort when you're not building the thing your mind keeps returning to. It pulls at you day and night. It interrupts your sleep. It overrides your fear. It drowns out the doubts, the naysayers, the endless reasons to quit. It becomes so entwined with your identity that the line between who you are and what you're building begins to blur.

This is the part people misunderstand. Obsession isn't a choice. It isn't a strategy. It isn't a mindset you adopt because a book told you to "hustle harder." It's the residue of everything that shaped you: the misfit years, the grinding against systems, the losses that tore you open, the shocking disloyalties that hardened you, the anger that demanded direction, the gifts no one recognized, the pain you survived, the emptiness you refused to drown in, and the relentless instinct that you were meant for something more. All of it fuses together and becomes a kind of internal gravity that pulls you toward your future whether you're ready or not.

For me, the pull only intensified once I began building LARC. There was no roadmap. There were no investors lining up with enthusiasm. There were no guarantees that this idea, this rebellious, unorthodox idea, would be accepted by an industry still clinging to its wooden relics with generational stubbornness. Most people assumed it was impossible. Some thought it was foolish. Many ignored it entirely.

But obsession allowed me to see the inevitability that others couldn't. It showed me the real truth hiding behind resistance: the greater the disbelief, the greater the opportunity. It's only when the world has accepted a broken system as normal that the stage is set for someone with a clear vision to rebuild it.

When I moved my family from California to Tennessee, chasing a place that aligned with my vision rather than suffocating it, the decision was pushed by obsession, not strategy. Tennessee offered something Silicon Valley couldn't: room to build, to breathe, to create something physical, real, necessary, without navigating a political and economic labyrinth designed to punish makers and reward talkers. But the move also revealed something deeper about obsession: it forces you to strip your life of anything that dulls your focus, understanding that environment, culture, and values matter, and if the world you're standing in can't support the weight of what you're trying to build, you must be willing to leave that world behind.

Meeting Chris Taylor happened in the same way everything else meaningful in my life has happened: through alignment, not luck. Chris was the kind of partner obsession recognizes immediately, grounded where I was intense, analytical where I was instinctual, pragmatic where I was impatient. He could see the beauty in the engineering challenge, while I saw the beauty in the destruction of an outdated paradigm. Together we formed a polarity that could actually bend reality. Every great company requires this kind of partnership, a collaboration between different forms of brilliance anchored by the same mission.

But obsession alone doesn't create sustainability. It creates motion, ignition, velocity. What sustains the journey is something deeper, something steadier, something rooted in faith and identity. And although she doesn't enter fully into this chapter yet, it's impossible to speak about the internal machinery of obsession without acknowledging the truth that would come later: even the most obsessive mind needs an anchor, someone who believes in you in ways you don't yet believe in yourself, who sees the madness not as a flaw but as raw fuel, who stands in the doorway of your life and steadies the storm rather than running from it. That, in my journey, would be my amazing wife Kate. But her entrance belongs to another chapter.

For now, Chapter Two is about the truth most people will never admit: obsession is the prerequisite to creation.

You can't build something that doesn't exist if you're not willing to lose sleep, sanity, comfort, stability, and sometimes the approval of everyone around you. You can't create a new industry by operating with the same level of desire as people who are content with maintaining the old one. And you can't change the world with anything less than an internal fire that borders on unreasonable, unbalanced, and at times unhealthy. Obsession is what allows you to hold the vision steady when everything else is shaking. When the market says no. When the industry says it can't be done. When people laugh. When suppliers hesitate. When the world responds to your clarity with uncertainty.

Entrepreneurs who build what doesn't exist aren't motivated by applause. They're compelled by inevitability. They're pulled forward by a vision so clear it might as well be memory. And they can't stop, even if they want to, because the alternative, staying small, staying silent, staying ordinary, would crush them far more painfully than the risks they take.

What I discovered as I built LARC, and what I want the reader to understand here, is that obsession isn't the enemy of balance. It's the enemy of mediocrity. It's the antithesis of stagnation. It's the one trait that separates those who talk about changing the world from those who actually do it.

And this is where I leave you at the end of Chapter Two:

If you feel restless, misaligned, misunderstood, if you can't quiet the internal noise telling you that the life you're living is too small for who you're becoming, good. That's obsession. And obsession, when aimed correctly, is the most powerful engine you'll ever possess. It's the current that will carry you through every collapse and every rebirth still to come.

Because building what doesn't exist requires something more than passion. It requires obsession.

And the story that follows is what obsession makes possible.

"Our doubts are traitors."

- William Shakespeare

3

The Quiet Violence of Doubt

The Internal Enemy

Doubt never announces itself boldly. It doesn't storm through the door or shout from the corners of your mind. It slips in almost politely, like an old acquaintance who knows your blind spots too well. Doubt waits for the moments when your energy dips, when your confidence wavers, when the world feels slightly heavier than usual, and then it speaks in a voice that sounds so much like your own that you don't immediately recognize it as the enemy.

For most people, doubt is an occasional visitor. It appears during big decisions or moments of stress, then fades as life returns to routine. But for entrepreneurs, especially the kind who build what doesn't yet exist, doubt is a constant presence. It's a companion, a shadow, a relentless whisper at the edge of every breakthrough. It's the internal resistance that activates not when you're failing, but precisely when you're rising.

Chapter Two explored obsession, the fire that drives you forward, the force pushing you toward creation. But what no one tells you is that obsession always wakes up its opposite. When you begin to build something extraordinary, the old identity inside you senses it's about to die. And identities don't die easily.

The world likes to talk about imposter syndrome as if it's a mild inconvenience, a motivational hurdle. But imposter syndrome isn't the real threat. The real threat is the version of you shaped by years of survival, years of misalignment, years of emotional warfare. When you begin to evolve into someone capable of building something meaningful, that old version fights back with precision. It knows your weaknesses better than any enemy ever will, because it grew up with you. It learned your fears before you could speak them. It learned your insecurities before you understood what insecurity meant.

This is the quiet violence of doubt: It's self inflicted, deeply familiar, and devastatingly accurate. For me, doubt didn't come from competitors, or advisors, or investors, or the industry skeptics who thought LARC was an impossible idea. My doubt came from somewhere far older. It came from the scars of childhood misalignment, from the mistrust shaped by emotional violation, from the silence left by a distant father, from the losses that carved out the interior of my life. It came from the kid who was told he didn't fit the system. It came from the teenager who had to rebuild too early. It came from the young man who learned the hard way that some people leave when you need them most.

Even after LARC began to take shape, after Chris joined the mission, after the first prototypes proved the idea wasn't madness, the old voice still returned with precision. Not in moments of failure, but in the quiet. The late nights. The early mornings. The pauses between victories. The silence after a breakthrough. Doubt thrives in stillness.

And the worst part is that it speaks in reason.

"Are you sure this is going to work?"
"You've rebuilt before, but what if this time you can't?"
"What if you're not as strong as you think?"
"What if you're wrong?"
"What if you push your family too far?"
"What if the betrayal wasn't just a moment, but a reflection of who you attract, who you trust, who you are?"

Doubt doesn't scream. It whispers.
And its whisper is more dangerous than any shout.

What people don't understand is that doubt is rarely about the present. It's about the past. It's the echo of every moment you were made small. Every time you were dismissed. Every time you were underestimated. Every moment you felt unworthy, unseen, misunderstood. Doubt is the ghost of the person you used to be trying to convince you that you haven't changed.

And for a long time, I listened. Even as LARC began gaining momentum, even as industries that had ignored me started paying attention, even as engineers, operators, and global firms started saying yes, doubt remained. It wrapped itself in the disguise of caution. It cloaked itself in the costume of realism. It posed as responsibility. But underneath every argument it made was a single, unspoken message: stay small. Doubt doesn't want to protect you. It wants to preserve the version of you that no longer exists.

When I moved to Tennessee and began building from the ground up, doubt was my most persistent visitor. I had clarity, but I also had ghosts. I had obsession, but I also had shadows. And every old wound found new ways to reassert itself when the pressure increased.

This is the part people never talk about. Building a company isn't hard because of the market or the competition or the logistics. It's hard because every step forward requires you to confront the parts of yourself you've spent years avoiding. Entrepreneurship isn't about idea execution. It's about psychological excavation.

You must tear out old wiring. You must confront old narratives. You must silence the voices that speak in your own tone. You must dismantle the protection mechanisms that once saved you but now confine you. You must rebuild your identity from the foundation up.

And that internal war, more than any business challenge you'll ever face, determines whether you build something extraordinary or collapse under the weight of the person you refuse to stop being. Because doubt doesn't just whisper. It hunts.

The Return of the Old Self

The most dangerous form of doubt isn't the kind that questions your idea. It's the kind that questions your identity. Ideas can be defended. Ideas can be adjusted. Ideas can be improved. But when doubt targets the self, when it reaches into the older, hidden layers of your mind and starts pulling at threads you thought you outgrew, that's when the internal war becomes existential.

For years, I believed that doubt was a mental obstacle I could think my way around, dissect, rationalize, or overpower with enough momentum. But doubt isn't logical. It doesn't operate at the surface. It doesn't care about your progress, your validation, your achievements, or the evidence you gather to prove your competency. Doubt moves in the subterranean parts of your psyche, those early formed, deeply embedded regions built long before you had any say in how you would see yourself. The parts formed in childhood, reinforced in adolescence, and cemented in the moments of trauma that marked the landscape of your life.

When I began building LARC in earnest, when the napkin sketch turned into CAD drawings, when the first prototypes began taking shape, when the early interest from industry giants flickered on the horizon, that's when the old version of myself returned with the most force. It sounds counterintuitive. You'd think doubt haunts the beginning, the unknown, the early fragility. But it doesn't. Doubt waits. It waits until the stakes rise. It waits until there's something to lose. It waits until the distance between who you were and who you are becomes threatening. And then it pounces.

The return of the old self is subtle at first. A thought here, a question there. Nothing that alarms you. Just enough to destabilize you. It asks if you're worthy of the momentum you're gaining. It reminds you of every failure, every mistake, every collapse. It resurfaces the imagery of old wounds not as memories, but as predictions. I found myself haunted by questions that seemed rational on the surface, but carried a sharp edge underneath. What if this version of success vanishes the way stability vanished when I was young? What if the people around me disappear like others have before? What if the foundation is as fragile as the ones that collapsed earlier in my life?

These questions weren't entrepreneurial doubts. They were emotional ones. They were the reflexive fears of the young version of me who learned that life could change violently in a single moment, that trust could be broken without warning, that safety was temporary, that stability was something other people were allowed to have, but not me. And while the man building LARC had the skill, the experience, the vision, and the team to push forward, the boy inside me, the one shaped by loss, dismissal, and early instability, was still unsettled.

This is the paradox of the builder: the adult leads the mission, but the child shapes the fears. And unless you confront the child's logic, you'll build with a split identity, one part racing toward the future, the other gripping the past with white knuckles.

When Chris joined me in Tennessee, steady, pragmatic, disciplined in ways that complemented the volatility of my intensity, the work accelerated. His presence sharpened ideas, grounded plans, and gave structure to the madness that obsession had begun. Together, we found a rhythm that made the impossible feel merely inconvenient. But even in that momentum, even in the presence of someone who believed in the mission as much as I did, doubt still found its openings. Doubt doesn't disappear when you find partners. Doubt simply changes its strategy.

With Chris at my side, doubt stopped attacking competency and started attacking certainty. It said that relying on anyone was dangerous. That sharing control was a risk. That trusting anyone fully might lead to the same abandonment, the same emotional wreckage that defined earlier chapters of my life. In its twisted logic, doubt insisted that self reliance was the only safe path, even though isolation had nearly destroyed me before.

This is what people don't understand: founders aren't driven by confidence but by contradiction, pulled forward by vision and pulled backward by memory, building with precision and doubting with intensity, moving boldly and fearing quietly. And if they don't learn to recognize the voice of their old self as an intruder, they'll mistake it for reason and obey it without question.

Every bold decision I made in those early days of LARC, every pitch, every design choice, every gamble, every negotiation with partners or suppliers, was accompanied by a parallel internal conflict. I could execute flawlessly while simultaneously questioning myself. I could build brilliantly while privately fighting the belief that it could all collapse.

The world sees the founder taking action. The founder sees the battles happening behind the action. And here's the truth: the doubt that hurts the most isn't the doubt that you'll fail. It's the doubt that you don't deserve to succeed. That's the brutal mental violence of it. Because it doesn't attack what you do. It attacks who you believe you are. And if you're not careful, if you don't detect the return of the old self quickly enough, doubt will infiltrate your decisions not with hesitation, but with sabotage.

It'll make you choose smaller opportunities. It'll make you avoid necessary risks. It'll make you overanalyze instead of act. It'll make you doubt your instincts, even though your instincts are the reason you survived, the reason you built, and the reason you're still standing at all.

For a long time, I thought doubt meant I was flawed. But what I eventually learned was far more revelatory: doubt means you're evolving. Doubt is the revolt created when the old self realizes it's being replaced. Doubt intensifies not because you're weak, but because you're winning the internal war. It's the death rattle of a version of you that can't come with you into the future you're building. Because if you want to build something extraordinary, you eventually must kill the voice that wants you small.

Killing the Voice That Wants You Small

There comes a point in every builder's life when the internal war can no longer remain a background conflict. You reach a threshold where the voice inside you that resists evolution becomes too loud, too familiar, too intrusive to ignore. It's in these moments, these psychological bottlenecks, that the real work of entrepreneurship begins. Because everything you build externally is a projection of what you've already built internally. And if the foundation inside you is unstable, the structure outside you will inevitably crack.

For me, that threshold arrived not in a moment of crisis, but in a time of transition. The early chaos of LARC was beginning to give way to traction. Conversations with major companies were shifting from curiosity to partnership. The engineering was sharper. The prototypes cleaner. The logistics model tighter. The team expanding. Chris and I were turning sketches into systems, systems into products, products into a paradigm shift. Everything pointed toward forward movement. And that's precisely when the old voice grew the loudest.

This is the part people rarely understand: the moment before a breakthrough is almost always the moment when doubt becomes most intense. Because the old identity, sensing its impending extinction, begins a final assault. It pulls from every memory, every wound, every misunderstanding, every failure, anything it can use as ammunition. It doesn't care about accuracy. It cares about survival. And its survival depends entirely on convincing you that you haven't changed.

Doubt shows you distorted versions of your past as proof that the future is unsafe. It reminds you of the teacher who underestimated you. It replays the nights when you felt invisible. It resurrects the injuries that marked your emotional history. It invokes the instability of early life, the grief of loss, the fear of abandonment. It weaponizes everything you endured, not to break you, but to keep you the same. Entrepreneurship is, at its core, the process of killing the identity built by your past so the identity built by your future can take its place.

That death isn't symbolic. It's psychological. It's emotional. It's spiritual. It's violent. The old self won't step aside willingly. It'll claw and scream and sabotage. It'll masquerade as logic, as caution, as humility, as realism. It'll claim to protect you. It'll dress itself in the voices of your parents, your old teachers, your critics, your fears, your failures. It'll use familiarity as its shield. And unless you recognize the deception, you'll obey it. You'll mistake its warnings for wisdom. You'll shrink when you should expand.

I spent years listening to that voice without questioning its legitimacy. Years believing that doubt was insight, that fear was prudence, that caution was wisdom. Years believing that emotional shadows were reality. But as LARC grew, as the mission became unmistakable, as the work began to matter on a scale larger than my past, the truth became undeniable: the voice of doubt wasn't the voice of reason. It was the voice of a self that had outlived its purpose.

The moment I finally understood this wasn't dramatic. There was no epiphany, no moment of revelation. It happened the way internal revolutions usually do, gradually, almost accidentally. I found myself one night staring at the whiteboard in our office, covered in new designs and I felt something shift. Not externally, but internally. A realization that the work in front of me was larger than the life behind me. A recognition that the boy who'd survived chaos, loss, and hardship had brought me far, but couldn't take me any farther.

It's a strange thing to realize you've outgrown yourself. What comes next is even stranger: deciding which parts of you deserve to survive the evolution. The rage? That stayed. It became fuel. The defiance? That stayed. It became resilience. The intolerance for inefficiency? That stayed. It became innovation. The rebellious instinct? That stayed. It became originality.

But the doubt, the voice that told me I was unworthy of success, unworthy of stability, unworthy of being believed in, unworthy of building something extraordinary, that had to die.

Killing that voice isn't an act of aggression. It's an act of liberation. It requires an understanding that the old self isn't your enemy but was your guardian during years when survival was the only mission, keeping you alive through trauma, through loss, through abandonment, protecting you when the world felt unsafe. That version of you served a purpose. But once the mission shifts from survival to creation, its strategies become chains. Its reflexes become limitations. Its warnings become sabotage. And the entrepreneur must choose: evolve, or remain trapped inside a self built for a life you no longer live.

That night, in front of that whiteboard, I made a decision so simple it almost felt trivial: I would stop listening to the voice inside me that wanted to keep me small. I would stop empowering the beliefs that belonged to a past version of me. I would stop mistaking fear for insight. I would stop interpreting emotional residue as evidence. I would stop allowing old wounds to shape new decisions. And in that decision, a decision no one saw, no one celebrated, no one knew existed, the trajectory of my life shifted. Because what I killed that night wasn't doubt itself. What I killed was its authority.

From that moment forward, doubt became data, not direction. It became a signal, not a command. It became something I examined, not something I obeyed. And most importantly, it became a reminder that evolution requires conflict, that in order to build what doesn't exist, you must first outgrow what already does.

This is the lesson I want the reader to take from this chapter: doubt isn't a sign you're unprepared. Doubt is a sign you're transforming. Doubt escalates when you're getting close to something real. Doubt intensifies because the old identity feels threatened. And doubt becomes violent because it senses that you're finally strong enough to live without it.

Entrepreneurs don't conquer doubt by eliminating it. They conquer doubt by outgrowing the version of themselves that generates it.

And once you cross that psychological threshold, once you stop letting the old self dictate the future, you become capable of creation on a scale you could never have imagined before. That's where LARC truly began to accelerate. That's when the mission crystallized. That's when the work stopped being a reaction to my past and started becoming a contribution to the future.

The violence of doubt doesn't end here. It never fully ends. But it loses its power. And what takes its place is something far more potent: clarity. Because the moment you kill the voice that wants you small, you finally have room for the voice that wants you extraordinary.

"Out of suffering have emerged the strongest souls;
the most massive characters are seared with scars."

- Kahlil Gibran

4

Scar Tissue

The Wounds That Shape the Builder

Before anyone ever becomes a founder, before the big ideas, before the prototypes, before the risk, the capital, the grind, there's something else. Something earlier. Something most people never acknowledge because it feels too vulnerable to name. Every real entrepreneur begins with a wound. Not a metaphorical one, not a poetic one, but a real psychological rupture that changes the slope of a life. A wound that shifts your relationship with safety, with uncertainty, with self reliance, with ambition. A wound that forces you to grow a layer of skin the world can't easily penetrate.

People like to imagine entrepreneurs as bold, fearless creators who begin with inspiration or opportunity or some brilliant insight scribbled into a notebook. But that's the sanitized version. The truth is far more complex. Builders, the ones who actually reshape the world, aren't born from comfort but from disruption, created in the heat of instability, their ambition not an extension of confidence but an adaptation to pain. Some people inherit security. Others inherit uncertainty. Entrepreneurs inherit the instinct to build because they had no choice but to construct themselves.

I didn't understand that truth when I was young. Back then, pain felt personal, arbitrary, punishing, undeserved. Losing my father as a teenager wasn't something I had the emotional maturity to interpret. It came without warning, without preparation, without the buffer of adulthood that helps soften the blow. One moment I was a kid who believed life was still flexible. The next, I was thrust into a version of responsibility and loneliness that no sixteen year old should have to carry. The world became heavier overnight. The future became something I had to navigate without a compass.

But even that loss wasn't fully understood until years later, when my mother, the person I was closest to, the person whose belief in me never wavered, fell ill and died less than a decade after my father. By then, I'd barely stabilized the emotional ground under my feet. Losing her was like losing the last piece of home. It wasn't grief that broke me; it was the combination of grief and the abrupt dissolution of stability. Pain layered on pain doesn't just add weight. It compounds it.

Those years left impressions that shaped everything that came later, the work ethic, the anger, the self reliance, the intolerance for weakness in myself, the distrust of systems that promised security but had never protected me, shaping how I built relationships, how I interpreted risk, how I calibrated ambition. And it created a soft but relentless message in my psyche: if I didn't build something stable, nothing in my life ever would be.

What I didn't know at the time was that this isn't unusual. When you study the lives of people who've built extraordinary things, not the ones with polished press releases, but the real builders, you find a pattern. The most transformative founders have one thing in common: early wounds became later superpowers. Their pain sharpened their perception. Their instability heightened their intuition. Their adversity became pattern recognition. Their losses gave them resilience that no training could replicate. Scar tissue, when it heals correctly, becomes stronger than the skin it replaces.

And so it was for me. The emotional chaos of my early life created a particular sensitivity, a way of reading people, situations, and environments with a depth that came from necessity. When you grow up with loss, you develop instincts others don't, learning to scan a room rapidly, sense danger before it becomes visible, anticipate patterns before others detect them, adapt, adjust, recalibrate, and create solutions instead of waiting for rescue.

Those instincts aren't academic. They're not taught through books or degree programs. They're earned in the aftermath of pain. But scar tissue doesn't form only from loss. It also forms from betrayal. And while I won't rehash what has already been addressed earlier in this book, I'll say this: nothing tests the integrity of your character like discovering that someone you trusted, deeply, and in a moment of vulnerability, wasn't who you believed them to be. Emotional betrayal leaves a scar unlike any other. It alters your relationship with trust. It sharpens your boundaries. It makes you more selective about who you let into your life. And, if you survive it, it creates a discernment that becomes a strategic advantage.

That period of my life didn't simply hurt. It reshaped me. It forced me into a level of self examination that few people ever face voluntarily. It demanded that I rebuild, not just my life, but my identity. The empty apartment floor didn't teach me anything new; it amplified what I'd ignored. It confronted me with the unmistakable truth that the person I'd been was no longer equipped to carry me forward. Scar tissue began to form there, not as a mark of damage, but as a signal of reconstruction.

This is what most people fail to understand: trauma doesn't create entrepreneurs; trauma reveals them. It exposes the mind's makeup. It exposes the internal wiring that refuses to surrender. It exposes the hunger that remains even when everything else collapses. Scar tissue doesn't weaken the entrepreneur. It strengthens the transition between who they were and who they must become.

Years later, when LARC began to take shape, not as a product, but as an idea, I could trace the instinct behind it to those early wounds. The refusal to accept inefficiency, the intolerance for systems that no longer worked, the insistence on building something fundamentally stronger, the relentless commitment to act even in uncertainty, those traits weren't skills I acquired; they were scars I'd repurposed. When I met Chris Taylor, with his Tennessee practicality and engineering clarity, there was an immediate recognition, two very different histories, two very different skill sets, but a shared trait: we both knew what it meant to build from nothing. His stability complemented my fire; my fire complemented his structure. That duality is what allowed LARC to evolve beyond a sketch into a system, beyond a system into a company, and beyond a company into a paradigm shift.

But the truth underlying all of it, the truth beneath the innovations, the designs, the engineering breakthroughs is that LARC was built by people who understood scarcity. People who were shaped by adversity. People whose scar tissue had turned into resolve.

Scar tissue isn't a badge of shame. It's the blueprint of resilience. And for entrepreneurs, it's the foundation on which everything else is built.

How Trauma Becomes Pattern Recognition, Instinct, and Power

Scar tissue doesn't arrive as strength. It arrives as pain. It arrives as confusion, as anger, as fear, as the question of whether you'll ever feel whole again. No one in the middle of heartbreak or loss or instability says, "This is making me stronger." That revelation only comes later, when you realize you've begun making decisions differently, not because you've become harder, but because you've become sharper.

Over time, wounds teach you to see the world with a level of clarity that comfort never could. Pain is a sculptor. It chisels away illusions, naivety, complacency, and wishful thinking. It exposes what's weak. It highlights what's real. It forces you to pay attention to signals most people never notice.

This is the first transformation of scar tissue: it becomes pattern recognition. People who've suffered, truly suffered, not the curated adversity that fills motivational speeches, develop an innate ability to sense patterns long before others see them. When you've lived through chaos, your nervous system becomes a radar for instability. You start noticing tone shifts in conversation. You detect hesitation where others hear confidence. You notice inconsistencies, red flags, misalignments, and micro changes in people's behavior. You recognize the early signs of disloyalty, and the subtle calculations behind manipulation, the signals that someone's words and actions don't match. You don't need time to learn people. You feel them.

In business, that instinct becomes a borderless advantage. It helps you choose the right partners. It helps you avoid catastrophic hires. It helps you navigate negotiations with clarity instead of hope. It helps you see around corners. And most importantly, it helps you build systems that withstand disruption, because you no longer operate under the illusion that stability is guaranteed.

For founders, scar tissue becomes a mapping system. It shows you where danger lives. It shows you where opportunity hides. It shows you how to assess risk with precision, because the consequences of miscalculation were once personal, not theoretical. That's why so many of the world's strongest entrepreneurs have difficult backgrounds, trauma doesn't teach you to fear the world; it teaches you not to trust it blindly. Trust, after trauma, is recalibrated. Not shut down. Not eliminated. Recalibrated.

You learn that trust isn't a default state; it's a currency. And you become extremely careful about where you spend it. You learn that loyalty isn't measured by words, but by presence. You learn that people who stand with you in darkness are worth more than those who applaud you in the light. You learn that true allies are rare, which makes them invaluable. And then something even more powerful happens: the very pain that once dismantled you becomes your engine.

Trauma changes your relationship with effort. People who've been protected from hardship often crumble under sustained pressure. Their threshold is low. Their tolerance for discomfort is fragile. Their belief in themselves is conditional on external validation. Those who learn to endure pain early develop a different and more powerful psychological muscle. They know how to keep moving even when their internal world is cracked open. They know how to function under emotional strain. They know how to survive things that break other people.

In entrepreneurship, that becomes resilience, the single most valuable trait a founder can possess.

Resilience isn't optimism. It isn't confidence. It isn't positivity. It's the ability to keep going when you have every reason to stop. It's the ability to hold a vision while the world gives you no evidence that it'll ever materialize. It's the ability to take hits without losing direction. It's the ability to be shattered and still move.

Scar tissue internalizes resilience. It gives you a tolerance for adversity most people never develop. You don't panic when things go wrong. You don't collapse when a deal falls through. You don't unravel when the market shifts. You don't overreact to noise. Pain gave you depth and stability. Stability gives you advantage. And then there's the other side of the coin: instinct.

Founders with scar tissue possess an instinct that isn't learned; it's inherited from experience. They see opportunities before others do because they know what inefficiency feels like. They know what dysfunction looks like. They understand human behavior without needing it explained. They can tell when something's off by watching how people stand, not what they say. They build products by focusing not on what customers ask for, but on what customers complain about, the pain points hidden beneath polite discourse.

Instinct isn't mystical. You've survived patterns enough times that your brain recognizes them without consciously processing the data.

This is why the companies built by scarred founders are often more robust. They're built by people who never assumed things would go right. And because they never assumed stability, they engineered resilience into the products. LARC is a perfect example. It wasn't built as a "nice to have" solution; it was built as a system designed to endure volatility. It was designed with a clear view of the problems the world overlooked. It was built by people who didn't see inefficiency as an inconvenience but as an insult. People who refused to accept "this is the way it's always been done" as a final answer. People who understood that innovation doesn't come from comfort. It comes from necessity. It comes from the refusal to let broken systems persist unchallenged. Scar tissue doesn't just create resilience, instinct, and pattern recognition. It creates hunger.

When you've lost enough, you don't fear losing again. When you've been broken, you don't fear breaking again. When you've rebuilt yourself once, you know you can rebuild yourself twice. Hunger is born from the knowledge that stability isn't a given, but something you construct. Something you earn. Something you maintain through force of will.

That hunger is what pushes founders to go further than competitors. It's what keeps them up late, thinking, sketching, designing, revising. It's what pushes them to take risks others avoid. It's what drives them to create momentum when resources are scarce. Hunger is the fire beneath innovation, and scar tissue keeps it burning.

This is the irony of trauma: it takes something from you, but if you survive it, it gives you something no one else can match. It gives you a psychological advantage that's impossible to replicate through education, wealth, or opportunity. It gives you the internal structure required not just to dream, but to endure.

People often talk about "founder DNA." What they really mean is scar tissue. Because in the end, the entrepreneurs who build the world don't succeed because they're fearless. They succeed because they've been afraid and kept moving anyway. They don't succeed because life was kind. They succeed because they learned to convert suffering into strength. They don't succeed because they were supported. They succeed because they learned to build support systems when none existed. Scar tissue is the architect of the entrepreneurial mind. And in the next section, we'll explore the most powerful truth of all: that the emotional wounds you spend years trying to hide may be the very thing that propels you to build the extraordinary.

The Identity Shaped by Adversity

Scar tissue isn't merely something you carry; eventually, it becomes who you are. It becomes the internal foundation from which decisions are made, instincts form, values crystallize, and leadership takes shape. By the time someone becomes a founder, truly becomes one, not by title but by temperament, their scar tissue has already written half the blueprint. The question is never whether a builder has scars. The question is whether they've learned how to wield them.

At some point, every entrepreneur is forced to confront the truth that the traits people admire in them, resilience, drive, intensity, decisiveness, hunger, weren't built by success. They were built by the years when nothing made sense, when survival depended on learning to read the world rapidly, when trust had to be earned, when hope had to be self generated, when comfort was a luxury and fear was a companion. These traits were born out of necessity long before ambition turned them into assets.

By the time I began building companies, before LARC, before Silicon Valley, before the logistics systems and the supply chain models, these traits were already operating beneath the surface. They shaped how I responded to pressure, how I approached conflict, how I assessed people, how I made decisions. I didn't learn these things in a classroom. I learned them because I had no choice.

When you lose a parent young, you develop emotional independence that most people never experience. When you lose the parent you were closest to, that independence calcifies. It becomes a way of moving through the world, self directed, self driven, self constructed. And when broken trust later collides with that foundation, it doesn't just break something; it transforms something. It strips away the last remnants of naivety and forces you into an accelerated form of adulthood. You become someone who studies people intently because you understand the cost of misjudgment. You become someone who relies heavily on instinct because you've already learned that words and appearances are often disguises. You become someone who values character above charm, loyalty above talent, presence above promises. That identity follows you everywhere, into relationships, into opportunities, and eventually into leadership.

When I began building LARC, I wasn't just designing crates. I was designing stability, designing protection, designing systems that wouldn't collapse under pressure. In many ways, the engineering philosophy mirrored the psychological philosophy scar tissue had already created in me: build it strong, build it intentionally, build it to withstand forces that most people don't anticipate. Build it in a way that doesn't rely on blind trust. Build it with clarity, precision, and resilience in mind. Build it with the expectation that pressure is coming. That mindset, the scar tissue mindset, is exactly what separated LARC from the thousands of startups around us. We weren't trying to create a cute product. We were creating a hardened system. We were engineering infrastructure. We were building something to endure.

When Chris joined the journey, something profound happened: he recognized the scar tissue in me, and I recognized the steadiness in him. Scar tissue, when integrated correctly, doesn't make you difficult to work with; it makes you discerning. And discerning people choose partners carefully. The shared drive was there, the operational difference was there, but the alignment of values, the shared belief in integrity, in grit, in doing things right, was what made the partnership real. Scar tissue informs who you trust, but it also informs who you can build with. And Chris became the structural counterweight to my fire, giving LARC the duality it needed to grow.

But the most important transformation scar tissue creates isn't in operational performance, it's in leadership. It changes not just what you build, but how you lead those building alongside you. It becomes the foundation of trust between founder and team.

Leaders who've been broken lead differently. They don't lead from ego. They don't lead from insecurity. They don't lead from fear. They lead from truth. They lead with stability, because they understand instability. They lead with empathy because they know the feeling of collapse. They lead with high standards because they've lived through the consequences of low ones. They lead with intensity because they know the stakes. They lead with clarity because they've already fought through confusion. And they lead with loyalty because they understand its rarity.

This is why the team at LARC became what it is today. Not because of motivational meetings or corporate culture decks, but because people with scar tissue can spot others with scar tissue. They recognize those who've been through something and made something of it. They know who'll show up when things get hard. They know who can take a hit. They know who can grind through the slow years. They know who can hold the line when everyone else is exhausted. Scar tissue recognizes scar tissue. And that recognition becomes the foundation of a team.

And then there's one final transformation scar tissue must complete, one that explains why any of this matters. Many founders never talk about this, because it feels too intimate, too revealing, even though it may be the most important truth of all. Scar tissue influences not just how you build companies, but how you build relationships, and ultimately, why you're building.

For years, I believed I needed no one. It wasn't arrogance; it was survival. When you've been forced to navigate life alone, asking for help feels unnatural. Letting someone support you feels dangerous. Trust feels like a luxury you can't afford. And vulnerability feels like a door you'd rather keep locked. That mindset is effective for endurance, but catastrophic for connection.

It wasn't until Kate came into my life that I understood the difference between being self reliant and being emotionally isolated. She didn't just lift me out of darkness; she showed me that building doesn't have to mean building alone. She showed me that real strength includes the courage to let someone stand beside you. She showed me that love isn't a weakness or something that would be used as a weapon against you, but a stabilizer. And she showed me that the right partner doesn't slow you down, they sharpen you, hold you accountable to your best self.

Scar tissue may create independence, but love, real, unwavering, battle tested love, teaches you interdependence. It teaches you that trust isn't naivety. It teaches you that faith isn't fragility. It teaches you that partnership isn't a compromise of self, but an elevation of it.

Kate was the first relationship in my adult life to prove that support doesn't always come at a price. That realization reshaped not just my personal world, but my entrepreneurial one. It taught me that choosing the right partner isn't just a romantic decision, though clearly that's vital; it's a strategic one.

But here's the revelation that an entrepreneur must accept above all else: scar tissue becomes identity, but identity isn't destiny. You choose what to do with what happened to you. You choose whether the wound becomes a weight or a weapon. You choose whether the trauma becomes a chain or a compass. You choose whether your scars define you or deploy you. Scar tissue isn't the reason entrepreneurs succeed. Scar tissue is the reason entrepreneurs can endure long enough to succeed.

Because in the end, every external breakthrough begins with an internal one. Every innovation begins with the decision to stop repeating patterns that once protected you but now limit you. Every act of creation begins with the belief that your future deserves more than your past. And every company that lasts, every company that matters, begins with a founder who learned to build from the materials life handed them, no matter how sharp the edges.

Scar tissue is the raw material of transformation. And the entrepreneurs who embrace it, fully, honestly, unapologetically, are the ones who eventually build what the world has never seen. But there's one final truth scar tissue reveals: at some point, you stop building for what lies ahead and start building for what stands behind you. You stop chasing ambition and start protecting what you can't bear to lose. Your scars taught you what truly matters. They taught you the difference between what you want and what you'd die for. They taught you that the deepest battles aren't fought for conquest, but for love.

This convergence of pain and purpose, this transformation of suffering into devotion, this is what I call the **Militant Mind**.

Built on scars. Driven by love.

This is how you build what doesn't exist. This is why you build at all.

"In solitude the mind gains strength
and learns to lean upon itself."

- Laurence Sterne

5

Isolation

The Solitude No One Warns You About

You build for love. But to build at all, you must first learn to stand alone.

There's a part of the entrepreneurial journey that almost no one speaks about openly, not because it's rare, but because admitting it feels like weakness. It isn't the grind, the pressure, the uncertainty, or even the fear. Those things are expected. The part that breaks people, the part they never see coming, is the isolation.

Isolation isn't a side effect of building. It's the crucible. It begins before the company exists, before the mission becomes real, before your name is attached to anything worth noticing. It arrives as distance, not loneliness. A widening gulf between you and everyone who still lives in the world you're leaving behind.

You start to notice that conversations feel hollow. The daily rhythms that once felt normal now feel suffocating. Your curiosity shifts toward ideas that are hard to articulate, fragile in their early form, and unwelcome in casual conversation. You begin living in a psychological landscape few people recognize, occupied by visions you can't yet prove and instincts you can't explain. This is the moment isolation takes hold. Not as emptiness, but as separation.

For many builders, it begins years before the first prototype. Looking back, I can see that it began in childhood for me. I was never the kid who blended in. I had a restless mind, a temper that flared when things didn't make sense, a natural aversion to rules that existed simply because someone said so. I understood even then that I was observing the world from a different angle. And that early sense of difference is often where entrepreneurial isolation is born.

But nothing prepares you for how that difference intensifies once you commit to building something real. What was once a subtle separation becomes an unbridgeable divide. You start making decisions others can't understand. You sacrifice things they consider sacred for outcomes they can't yet see. And slowly, inevitably, you realize that the mission has claimed you in ways you never agreed to but can't reverse.

When I first started creating companies, I didn't have a name for what I felt. I just knew I needed more silence than before. More space to think. More room to let ideas breathe. My mind was accelerating while the world around me moved at the same pace it always had. I found myself stepping out of conversations mentally, drifting elsewhere, into the landscape of problems I wanted to solve, ideas I wanted to test, systems I wanted to build. It wasn't disconnection; it was immersion. I wasn't withdrawing from the world. I was entering another one.

It was in the silent hours, the mornings before the house woke, the nights after the noise died, that I felt the space necessary to build something that mattered. Isolation placed me alone with my thoughts in a way no meeting or conversation ever could. It stripped away distraction. It removed the pressure to perform. It made me accountable only to the vision forming inside my own mind.

In isolation, you discover what you actually believe. You discover whether your ideas can withstand scrutiny. You discover your weaknesses before the world does. You discover the line between ambition and delusion. You discover whether your resolve is real or borrowed. These truths don't come from mentors or books. They come from silence. People mistake isolation for loneliness, but for builders, they're not the same. Loneliness is the absence of connection. Isolation is the presence of creation. It's the space where the next version of you is under construction.

In those early years, as LARC evolved from napkin sketch to engineered system, isolation became where the work hardened. I spent nights alone in empty rooms, sketching designs, reworking calculations, mapping logistics flows, questioning whether the world was ready for what I was building. No one else could carry that phase. It belonged to the part of me that had always operated at the edge of the familiar.

Isolation sharpens the mind in ways nothing else can. The absence of noise forces you to confront your thoughts with brutal honesty. There's no audience to perform for, no feedback loop to soften the blow, no validation to hide behind. What remains is your raw relationship with the work. And that relationship determines whether your vision survives or dies.

Isolation reveals the chasm between the life you knew and the life you're building. When you move into new territories of ambition, you realize that most people won't understand what you're doing, not because they lack intelligence, but because they don't feel what you feel. They don't experience the same pressure. They don't see the patterns you see. They don't feel the urgency. They're not meant to. If they were, they'd be building beside you.

This is the truth most founders deny too long: you can't bring everyone with you. The path narrows as the vision sharpens. Friendships drift. Conversations fade. Routines dissolve. Identities disappear. It's not rejection. It's not conflict. It's evolution. And evolution is always solitary.

Isolation teaches you to trust your internal compass over external noise. It teaches you that clarity doesn't come from consensus. It teaches you that breakthroughs aren't social events. They're private wars fought in the hours when no one is watching. This is the narrowing.

The place where rough ideas become structure. The place where uncertainty becomes direction. The place where the old self dissolves and the new identity is hammered into form. The place where the entrepreneur emerges.

Where Instinct Sharpens and Faith Is Born

Isolation isn't just a condition of the entrepreneurial journey. It becomes the environment where instinct sharpens into something nearly primal. When you spend enough time in true silence, not the casual quiet of a slow afternoon but the internal stillness that arrives when there's no one to validate your decisions and no one to applaud your progress, you begin to hear what was always there but never audible.

In the early stages of building LARC, the isolation felt like a pressure chamber. The world wasn't watching, and that was a blessing disguised as obscurity. Without external noise, my mind began to speak in a clearer voice. Ideas that once felt chaotic began falling into place. Problems that felt overwhelming became solvable. Pathways that seemed impossible began to reveal themselves through patterns I never would've noticed in a louder life.

This sharpening of instinct isn't magic. It's the inevitable result of sustained focus. When you sit long enough with a problem, when you replay it, rethink it, break it apart, rebuild it, you start to develop an intuitive sense of direction. You start anticipating outcomes without consciously analyzing them. You begin to make decisions that feel instantaneous but are actually the culmination of thousands of hours of private thought.

Isolation transforms the mind into an instrument tuned to a single frequency. And in that space, something else emerges. Something most founders never admit out loud because it sounds too vulnerable, too soft, too unquantifiable for the world of business.

Faith

Faith is born in silence. Not blind hope. Not wishful thinking. Real faith. The kind that comes from confronting the void where answers should be and continuing to move forward anyway. Isolation forces you to recognize the limits of your control. You can design, prepare, plan, strategize, engineer, but eventually you arrive at the boundary where human certainty ends. Most people panic at that edge. Entrepreneurs learn to step off it. That step is faith.

You don't grow faith when everything is clear. You grow it when clarity disappears. You grow it when you're designing systems for an industry that has never seen them. You grow it when you're pitching ideas people can't yet visualize. You grow it when you're working in the dark with nothing but conviction as your guide. You grow it when the only evidence your idea might work is the fact that you can't silence the belief that it will. Isolation becomes the incubator of that belief.

There were nights when the future of LARC lived only in my head, fragile enough to crumble under the wrong conversation, strong enough to keep me awake with ideas I couldn't ignore. In those nights, faith wasn't optional. It was oxygen. It was the force that kept me moving when uncertainty was absolute. I realized in those hours that faith isn't something you inherit. It's something you build, piece by piece, from every silent moment you refuse to quit. And once faith takes root, once it becomes the operating system beneath every decision, isolation begins shaping something else. Your capacity to endure.

Entrepreneurship demands a level of endurance the average person never experiences. It isn't purely intellectual. It's physical. It's emotional. It's chemical. Long hours. Stress cycles. High stakes. Constant decisions. These forces place a load on the body as much as the mind, and founders who neglect their physical state eventually pay the price. In the same way that silence strengthens clarity, physical discipline strengthens resolve.

For me, staying physically fit wasn't a hobby or a vanity metric. It became part of my operating system. The gym was one of the few places where the noise fell away. Training forced my mind into presence, into breath, into movement. It stabilized my nervous system, cleared my thinking, and created a buffer between me and the weight of the work. Physical discipline became the counterpart to isolation. One sharpened the mind, the other fortified the body, together they sustained the long stretches where support was nonexistent.

Entrepreneurs often underestimate the degree to which their bodies amplify or sabotage their minds. Fatigue can masquerade as doubt. Stress can disguise itself as caution. Hormonal imbalance can present as fear. A weakened body becomes a gateway for a weakened mission. But when you train your body, you're also training your endurance, your ability to handle pressure, your tolerance for discomfort, your capacity to stay focused when others break.

And in that space, the founder begins to evolve into something more precise. The noise falls away. The instincts sharpen. The faith strengthens. The capacity grows. The vision clarifies. Isolation is no longer something you endure. It becomes something you seek, something you rely on, something you trust. Because in the stillness, you begin hearing the faint outlines of the future you're building, long before anyone else recognizes its shape.

Most people fear isolation because they associate it with abandonment or emptiness. But founders learn a different definition. Isolation becomes a laboratory. A sanctuary. A training ground. A place where ideas are born without interference and decisions are made without dilution. It becomes the environment where you finally meet the version of yourself capable of leading the mission ahead. And in the next part of this chapter, we'll push even deeper into the transformation, into how isolation forces the ego to break, how it clarifies purpose, and how it gives birth to the kind of leadership the world rarely sees but always needs.

Where Ego Breaks and Purpose Emerges

An entrepreneur must be bold enough to believe it and humble enough to do it, and nowhere does that truth reveal itself more painfully or more profoundly than in isolation. Solitude strips away every illusion you've built around yourself. It forces you to sit with the parts of your identity you prefer to avoid. The ego, which thrives on noise and comparison and external markers of progress, begins to suffocate in stillness. It can't hide behind activity. It can't posture behind confidence. It can't inflate itself on results that haven't happened yet. In isolation, there's only you, your ambition, your flaws, your fears, your intentions, your beliefs, and the distance between the person you are and the person you're becoming.

When the world falls silent, the ego cracks. The fracture isn't violent; it's revealing. You begin to see with brutal clarity the ways your ego used to negotiate with your dreams, the ways it tried to make ambition more comfortable, the ways it lied to you under the guise of practicality or caution or timing. You notice how often ego tried to take shortcuts, to avoid responsibility, to cling to old identities that no longer fit. And you realize that ego was never the engine. It was the resistance.

Isolation exposes that resistance. It shows you the parts of yourself that prefer applause over accountability. It reveals how much of your past ambition depended on being seen, not on being true. And once you've faced those truths long enough, the ego loses its authority. Its grip loosens. Its voice weakens. Its demands become recognizable as distractions rather than directives. With ego diminished, precision takes its place.

Your thinking sharpens. Your intentions clarify. Your standards rise. The mission detaches from your need to look like a founder and becomes rooted instead in the responsibility to build something real. Silence becomes the mirror in which the work can finally reflect back without distortion. You begin to understand that leadership isn't about being the loudest voice in the room. It's about being the clearest one. And clarity is a product of humility, not ego.

This humility doesn't look like self deprecation or modesty. It looks like commitment. The humble builder is the one who shows up when no one is watching. The one who works when there's no recognition. The one who questions their own assumptions. The one who adapts instead of defending outdated ideas. Humility isn't weakness. It's the internal structure that supports massive ambition without collapsing under the weight of it.

Isolation is the environment where humility becomes strength. It's where you begin to separate what you want your work to be from what your work actually is. It's where the mission becomes more important than your image, where solutions become more important than validation, where progress becomes more important than pride. When the ego finally quiets, you can hear the deeper voice beneath it, the voice of purpose. That voice is steady. It's not reactive. It doesn't seek applause. It seeks alignment.

The early years of LARC made this lesson unavoidable. I would sit alone for hours, surrounded by sketches, materials, prototypes, that were evolving faster than funding, and problems that demanded solutions no one had ever attempted before. There was no one to impress in those nights. There was no one to reassure me that the idea was brilliant or that the direction was right. There were no handshakes, no meetings, no headlines. Just the work and the weight of it.

In those hours, ego had nothing to offer. Only humility made the difference. The humility to revise, rethink, rethink again, and then rethink again. The humility to accept when something wasn't good enough. The humility to scrap the wrong path and rebuild from scratch. The humility to recognize that the mission required a higher version of me than the one who began it.

Isolation is the space where you become that higher version. It's also where leadership begins to take shape. True leadership isn't built in crowds. It's built in stillness. When you've spent enough time alone with your doubts, fears, and flaws, you develop a steadiness that others instinctively trust. You become less reactive, less fragile, less concerned with appearances. You stop leading from insecurity and start leading from conviction. You stop chasing control and start embracing responsibility.

The founders who lead well are the ones who made peace with themselves in silence long before anyone followed them.

Eventually, isolation evolves from something you must endure to something you return to by choice. It becomes your laboratory, your sanctuary, your calibration chamber. When the noise outside grows too loud, investors, customers, deadlines, expectations, you go back to the stillness because that's where your instincts sharpen, where your purpose anchors, where your direction realigns. Silence becomes the place where the next stage of the mission begins long before the world sees it.

Isolation teaches you that success isn't built in rooms crowded with people. It's built in rooms where you stood alone and did the work anyway.

This is why so many entrepreneurs fail. Not because they lack intelligence or talent, but because they can't withstand the solitude required to become the person their mission demands. They want the momentum without the silence. They want the breakthrough without the breakdown of ego. They want the clear vision without the quiet. They want the transformation without the time alone required to shed the version of themselves that can't survive the next level.

Isolation isn't a temporary phase. It's a discipline, a tool, a companion. It's the forge where the builder becomes the founder, where the founder becomes the leader, and where the leader becomes the architect of something that didn't exist before.

And now, having crossed the silent threshold, you're ready for the next evolution of the militant mind: the harnessing of the darker forces, the anger, the fear, the fire, that most people run from but founders learn to weaponize.

"No tree, it is said, can grow to heaven
unless its roots reach down to hell."

- Carl Jung

6

Rage and Fire: Using "Dark" Energy Properly

The Energy No One Wants to Admit They Use

People have always looked at me a certain way. They've called me intense. They've called me blunt. They've called me sharp. And more times than I can count, they've called me angry. Sometimes they say it carefully, as though they're stepping near something volatile. Sometimes they say it jokingly, like they're trying to soften the truth they don't fully understand. And sometimes they say nothing at all, but their eyes say it for them.

He's angry.

What they rarely understand is that anger isn't the poison. It's the signal.

From a young age, I felt things strongly. Injustice. Inefficiency. Dishonesty. Waste. Arrogance. Stupidity. The feeling of being underestimated. The feeling of being constrained. The feeling of being told to stay within lines that made no sense. My mind reacted to those things with heat, not apathy. With intensity, not passivity. With defiance, not compliance. The world wanted me calm, agreeable, linear. But nothing in me was built that way.

And instead of seeing that anger for what it really was, raw energy, unrefined potential, the unshaped fire of a builder, the world decided to label it as a flaw. As a problem to fix. As something to suppress. Teachers told me to calm down. Coaches told me to control myself. Adults told me to be less reactive, less opinionated, less sharp, less everything. They didn't understand that the anger wasn't about disruption. It was about recognition. I saw things they didn't. I felt things they ignored. I reacted to the world not as it was presented, but as it truly was.

Anger was my early warning system.

But here's the problem: if anger isn't understood, it becomes destructive. If you don't learn how to channel it, it turns inward. It becomes resentment, bitterness, cynicism, self sabotage. It becomes a constant friction that doesn't push you forward but holds you back. And that's what happens to most people. They fear their own fire. They learn to suppress the thing that could've been their fuel.

They fear their anger so much that they bury it. And in burying it, they bury their ability to see the world with the sharpness required to change it.

Entrepreneurs are different. Or at least, the ones who survive long enough to build something meaningful are different. They learn, often through painful trial, to stop apologizing for that internal fire and instead start shaping it. They learn that anger isn't the enemy. It's the raw material.

People often assume that the calmest leaders are the strongest ones, but anyone who's been in the trenches knows the truth: the leaders who build revolutions, the leaders who create new categories, the leaders who change industries are the ones whose fire never died. Their anger didn't disappear. It transformed. Because anger, when understood and harnessed, becomes far more than emotion. It becomes data. It becomes direction. It becomes the clearest indicator of misalignment.

Anger tells you where a system is broken. Anger tells you where something is unjust. Anger tells you where inefficiency is suffocating progress. Anger tells you where complacency is rotting potential. Anger tells you that you're seeing something others refuse to confront. People thought I was angry because I was unstable. In truth, I was angry because I saw clearly.

And the more I grew, the more I realized that anger was simply one part of a larger constellation of dark energy. Fear, frustration, intensity, rage, restlessness. The unfiltered emotional electricity that lives inside people who are wired for more than the world around them. Most people spend their lives trying to extinguish those emotions. Founders learn that they're not meant to extinguish them, but to refine them.

Fear becomes vigilance. Rage becomes fuel. Intensity becomes focus. Frustration becomes innovation. Restlessness becomes momentum. The transformation only happens when you stop allowing dark energy to control you and start using it as propulsion.

The world is uncomfortable with this idea because it prefers a sanitized version of success. It wants ambition without aggression. Vision without intensity. Drive without disruption. Passion without pressure. It wants builders to be inspirational but never threatening, confident but never forceful, bold but never confrontational.

That's not how real change happens. That's not how industries evolve. That's not how companies survive. It's certainly not how anything extraordinary gets built.

When I founded LARC, it wasn't a calm desire to improve packaging that drove me. It was fury. Fury at inefficiency. Fury at waste. Fury at the archaic systems that gigantic industries were still using. Fury at the idea that two million dollar server racks, the backbone of the digital world, were being encased in wooden boxes that wouldn't have impressed an Egyptian embalmer four thousand years ago. The anger wasn't irrational. It was accurate. It wasn't negativity. It was clarity. I wasn't furious because I wanted to burn things down. I was furious because things needed to change and no one else seemed willing to force the issue.

That's the part people misunderstand about founders who carry fire in their chest. Our anger is almost never about ego. It's about vision. We see the world not as it is, but as it should be. And the gap between those two realities creates heat. That heat, if harnessed, becomes power.

When Chris came into the picture, part of what made our partnership work was that he understood the fire without being afraid of it. He didn't mistake intensity for instability. He didn't misinterpret anger as misdirection. He saw what the dark energy was fueling. And he brought a form of steadiness that allowed the fire to stay controlled. That's the balance great companies require. One person who sees the future before it arrives and another who helps anchor the trajectory.

But long before I had anyone to help channel it, I had to learn the hard way that dark energy doesn't disappear with age. It doesn't fade. It doesn't dissolve. It matures. It condenses. It becomes denser. You learn to carry it differently. You learn to aim it rather than leak it. You learn to convert it into motion rather than destruction.

And that's what this chapter is about: the alchemy of turning fire into force. Because the truth is simple: every founder carries darkness. Some pretend they don't. Some hide it. Some fear it. But the ones who build what the world has never seen are the ones who turn their darkness into drive.

The Alchemy of Turning Heat Into Direction

The moment dark energy begins to transform is never loud. It doesn't happen in some dramatic explosion of clarity or in a single sweeping revelation. It happens gradually, almost invisibly at first. One day you realize that the anger isn't flaring out in every direction anymore. It's narrowing. It's sharpening. It's finding targets instead of victims. It's becoming directional rather than reactive. That's the alchemy.

Most people imagine anger as something wild and uncontrollable, a kind of internal storm that tears through everything around it. For many, that's exactly what it becomes, because they never learn to understand it. They never learn that beneath anger sits information. Beneath rage sits clarity. Beneath intensity sits truth. The fire they carry is trying to tell them something, not about the world, but about themselves.

What founders eventually figure out is that dark energy is a signal pointing toward misalignment. Rage doesn't come from nowhere. It sparks when your vision outgrows your current environment. It surges when your potential is constrained. It ignites when incompetence stands in your way. It grows white hot when someone underestimates you or disrespects your work or treats your ambition like a hobby. That level of intensity doesn't appear in people who are content where they are. It appears in those who are being called to something larger.

People who've never felt this will mistake it for volatility. People who've felt it but lack discipline will mistake it for justification. But the builder learns to see it as something else entirely: guidance.

The shift happens the first time you stop reacting outward and instead start asking inward, "What is this anger showing me?" The first time you stop interpreting fear as a threat and start interpreting it as a map. The first time you sit with frustration long enough to realize it's pointing directly at the thing you're meant to solve.

I remember a distinct period before LARC took shape, a period where my anger felt almost constant. If I walked into a warehouse and saw multimillion dollar equipment shoved into wood boxes, I felt fury. If I watched companies bleed money on logistics inefficiency, I felt irritation. If I saw the same outdated systems accepted as normal, I felt pressure in my chest. It wasn't because I wanted to complain. It was because I could see the solution before anyone else did. And the gap between my vision and their acceptance drove me mad. But that madness was actually alignment. Dark energy pointed me to the precise place where I was meant to build.

Fear works the same way. People see fear as weakness, but that's only because they've never examined it carefully. Fear is information. It tells you where the stakes are highest. It tells you where your growth lives. It tells you what matters to you more than comfort. That's why the things that terrify you are often the things that matter most. Fear isn't a sign you're off track. It's a sign you're standing at the frontier of breakthrough.

Every founder, at some point, sits with fear in the dark. Fear of failure. Fear of being exposed. Fear of being wrong. Fear of building something that doesn't work. Fear of leading people and letting them down. Fear of aiming too high. Fear of aiming too low. Fear of wasting time. Fear of wasting talent. Fear of becoming the version of yourself you always feared you might be.

But the founder learns something the average person never does: fear is most powerful when you move toward it rather than away from it. Once you start doing that, once you stop interpreting fear as a wall and start interpreting it as a doorway, something shifts inside you. The fear doesn't disappear. It becomes fuel.

This same transformation happens with rage. Rage is raw potential. It carries more energy than motivation ever will. Rage is unfiltered conviction that something is broken and must be fixed. People who lack rage lack fire. People who lack fire rarely build anything that lasts. But rage must be aimed. Unaimed rage is destruction. Aimed rage is revolution. The moment you give your fire a target, a mission, a problem, a vision, a company, the wildness becomes power. The chaos becomes strategy. The heat becomes momentum.

Dark energy becomes the most reliable fuel in your arsenal not because it's pleasant or beautiful, but because it never runs out. Motivation burns away, passion flickers, excitement fades, and inspiration appears only in unpredictable bursts, but dark energy remains steady beneath it all. It resurfaces when you're exhausted, when you're underestimated, when you meet resistance, when the world dismisses you, and especially when someone looks you in the eye and says, "That'll never work."

People often assumed my anger meant I was unstable. They never understood it was the very thing that made me unstoppable. Anger without direction is immaturity, but anger given a target becomes innovation. Fear without courage is paralysis, but fear paired with forward motion becomes progress. Intensity without discipline is chaos, but intensity channeled with precision becomes dominance.

This is the transformation every founder must eventually undergo, the shift from being ruled by emotional electricity to deliberately running that electricity through the circuitry of purpose. And next, we'll dive into how that energy, once understood and shaped, becomes a durable propulsion system that carries you forward long after motivation dies, long after the odds turn against you, and long after everyone else has quit.

The Conversion to Controlled Burn

I went to Fairfax High School in Los Angeles, the same school Anthony Kiedis and Flea from the Red Hot Chili Peppers came out of. If you grew up there, you couldn't avoid their influence. They were woven into the identity of the place. Raw, rebellious, sharp edged, unapologetically themselves. And years later, long after I left those halls behind, I remember hearing their song "Dark Necessities" and stopping cold. The lyrics carried a message most people never hear: the darkness inside you isn't an enemy. It has a purpose. It has direction. It has something to teach you. It's a necessity, not because it feels good, but because without it, you never evolve into who you're meant to become.

That idea lodged itself in me in a way few things ever have, because it captured what most of the world refuses to understand: your darkness is part of your architecture. The fire inside you, the anger, the intensity, the fear, the restlessness, isn't something to run from, but something to refine. And the moment you stop trying to extinguish it and instead begin to shape it is the moment everything changes.

That turning point doesn't happen in flashes of revelation or dramatic breakthroughs. It happens gradually, through repeated confrontations with yourself. Eventually you begin to see that your anger is simply energy reacting to misalignment, your fear is energy reacting to importance, and your intensity is energy reacting to potential. Once you understand that, the fire stops burning you from within and starts burning away whatever holds you back.

Controlled burn is the stage entrepreneurs must reach if they want to build anything meaningful. It's one of the most misunderstood states of the founder's psyche. People romanticize clarity, imagining it as calm, steady, and serene. But for many builders, real clarity is made in heat. Focus becomes a byproduct of fury properly directed. Discipline becomes a container strong enough to hold intensity without letting it spill into chaos. You learn to aim the fire, not suppress it. You feel the same heat you always did, but now it has boundaries, direction, and purpose. It becomes a resource instead of a liability.

This is the point where founders begin to separate from everyone else. Not because they possess supernatural intelligence or talent, but because they have more internal fuel than the average person and finally know how to use it. Most people rely on motivation, a fragile thing that evaporates the moment life becomes difficult. But founders who reach controlled burn operate on a deeper current. They keep going not because they feel inspired, but because they feel compelled. They don't wait for good days. They move through the bad ones. They navigate storms that paralyze others, because they're no longer fighting themselves. They're leveraging themselves.

My own shift became clear in LARC's early years, during the long stretches when progress demanded more endurance than hope. There were days so heavy the air felt thick. Days when pressure fused with exhaustion. Days when doubt sat on my chest like a boulder. But something in me kept burning, steady and relentless. The anger at inefficiency, the frustration with outdated systems, the visceral rejection of mediocrity, all of it settled into a focused drive that didn't waver. I learned that if I put the mission at the center of the fire, the fire would keep pushing me forward. My dark energy stopped scattering outward and began flowing in a single direction: through the work.

And that's the revelation founders eventually reach. Your darkness isn't separate from your success. It's woven into the frame. Rage becomes the courage to challenge what no one else will. Fear becomes the urgency to evolve. Intensity becomes the stamina to endure what would break most people. The fire people think of as a flaw becomes your advantage. People used to call me angry, and they meant it as an indictment. What they never saw was that anger, once sharpened, became vision. They mistook heat for instability because they couldn't recognize it as fuel.

Once the fire becomes controlled burn, the world begins calling you disciplined instead of angry, driven instead of confrontational, focused instead of volatile. You didn't become softer. You became sharper. You didn't lose your heat. You just stopped wasting it. And discipline is nothing more than the structure that allows intensity to work in your favor.

At this point, you no longer waste your fire on insignificant battles. You stop reacting to every slight or distraction. You stop allowing your energy to scatter in a hundred directions. The mission becomes the magnet, and everything else falls away. You learn that not everything deserves your fire. Only the things you're willing to burn for.

That's the true purpose of dark energy: to reveal what matters, strip away what doesn't, and fortify what must endure. It's not meant to make you pleasant. It's meant to make you effective. It's not meant to make you easy. It's meant to make you unstoppable. It's not meant to make you blend in, but make you capable of building something the world has never seen.

This chapter isn't about glorifying anger or romanticizing intensity. It's about accepting that the internal fire most people suppress is the same fire that builders, creators, and founders learn to shape. It's about recognizing that your darkness doesn't disqualify you. It prepares you. It's part of your wiring, part of your resilience, part of the engine that powers everything you'll build.

And it's the bridge into the next chapter, the moment where the fire you harness must face its ultimate opponent: the old version of yourself that refuses to die quietly. Because once the darkness becomes fuel, the next battle isn't with the world, but with the parts of you that still want to stay small.

"Rejection is nothing more than a redirection;
a course correction to your destiny."

- Bryant McGill

7

When the World Say No

The Season of Invisibility

Every entrepreneur eventually enters a season where the world refuses to see them. For some, it happens early. For others, it arrives later, just when they thought they were finally breaking through. But it always arrives. There's always a chapter where the world says no. Not loudly. Not violently. Often not even intentionally. It's more low-key than that. More passive. More suffocating. It shows up as unanswered emails, unreturned calls, hollow promises, polite rejections, deflected meetings, stalled conversations, gatekeepers who smile at you while locking the door behind them, people who say "interesting" as a way of saying "never," and the slow, grinding disappearance of validation.

If you stay in this game long enough, you'll learn something painful and permanent: most of your early journey will be spent in a long corridor of invisibility. A corridor where no one believes in your vision, or worse, no one cares. You'll knock and knock, but the door won't open. You'll speak clearly, but no one hears you. You'll show the roadmap, the metrics, the prototypes, the conviction, and the world will shrug. It's not personal, though it'll feel that way. It's simply that people rarely recognize beginnings. They only see momentum once it's undeniable.

Founders like to talk about their breakthroughs, their big deals, their press moments, their victories. They rarely talk about the endless stretch of silence that came before it. The private battles. The humiliating meetings. The forced optimism. The rehearsed confidence. The lonely drives home. The car parked in silence after yet another rejection, wondering how many more hits you can take before you fall apart. The world sees the moment you're discovered, but it never sees the years you wandered.

When I was building LARC in the early days, the silence was deafening. There were years when nothing moved. Years where I felt like I was screaming through glass, pounding on a wall while the world moved on without me. Logistics isn't sexy. Packaging isn't glamorous. No one wakes up eager to hear about crate design. And yet I knew the industry was broken. I knew the solutions were outdated. I knew the companies relying on wood were bleeding money and wasting resources. The world needed something different, something engineered, something built for the next century instead of the last. But knowing and being believed aren't the same thing.

I walked into meeting after meeting where people would listen politely, nod along, and then escort me out with the same empty phrase: "We'll be in touch." They never were. I pitched companies that would later become customers, massive, global names, and back then, they couldn't hear me. Not because the idea wasn't good. Not because the need wasn't real. But because the world is conditioned to trust what already exists and distrust what doesn't.

Entrepreneurs forget this: you're asking people to believe in a future that only you can see. You're asking them to step into a reality that has no evidence yet. You're presenting something that hasn't proven itself. And human beings are wired to fear uncertainty more than they fear loss. This means the world will almost always say no long before it ever says yes.

And here's the part no one prepares you for: the world doesn't reject you dramatically. It rejects you softly. It ignores you. It doubts you. It questions your sanity. It belittles your vision in subtle ways. It suggests you should aim lower. It frames your ambition as arrogance. It implies you're unreasonable. It gives you advice dressed as discouragement. It hides its fear behind practicality. It confuses its own lack of imagination with your lack of feasibility. This isn't because people are cruel. It's because most people can't see past the edges of their own experience.

The rejection hurts, yes. But the invisibility is worse. Rejection at least acknowledges your existence. Invisibility erases you. It steals the oxygen from your lungs. It makes you question whether you're delusional. It makes you wonder if the universe is trying to tell you something, if maybe the vision you have isn't a calling but a hallucination.

There were nights during LARC's early stages when I would lie awake staring at the ceiling, wondering if I was the only one who saw it. The inefficiency. The waste. The archaic systems. The opportunity. I could see the entire industry years into the future. I could see modularity, reusability, engineered systems, full cycle logistics, the death of wood, the rise of sustainable platforms for high value cargo. But no one was ready for that conversation. Companies were still thinking in spreadsheets instead of ecosystems, still patching holes in their supply chains instead of rebuilding the foundation. They weren't ready for the future I was already standing inside.

That's the curse of a founder: you see what others can't yet imagine, and you feel what others can't yet sense. You're living in the next chapter while everyone else is still clinging to the previous one. And until the world catches up, you'll walk alone.

These seasons of invisibility aren't detours. They're part of the process. They're where founders either break or become unbreakable. They expose whether your vision is real or just romantic. They test your endurance. They sharpen your instincts. They force you inward. They demand you build a spine strong enough to carry the weight of a future no one else wants to hold with you. And they teach you something brutal but necessary: the world's validation is a late arrival.

Entrepreneurs often assume rejection means they're wrong. But what if it means they're early? What if the no you receive today is simply the inability of someone else to see the world you're already operating in? What if the silence isn't a sign of your inadequacy, but a sign that you're building something that doesn't yet have a category or a language? Being early feels exactly like being wrong until the world catches up.

Every great company began as an idea that looked ridiculous. Amazon looked absurd. Airbnb looked foolish. SpaceX looked delusional. The entire early internet looked like a toy. People mocked electric cars. People dismissed streaming. People laughed at the idea of reusable rockets. What these stories have in common isn't brilliance. It's endurance. When the world said no, the founders didn't shrink. They expanded. They held the vision long enough for the world to develop the vocabulary to understand it. The world won't give you permission. You take it by surviving long enough.

The worst part of these seasons isn't the rejection itself but the loneliness it creates. People will support you in theory but distance themselves in practice. Investors will say they love your story but not enough to place a bet. Friends will say they believe in you but wonder silently why you haven't made it yet. You'll begin to feel the isolation tightening around you like a grip, and if you're not careful, it'll crush your belief. Most people quit here. They don't fail because of bad ideas or bad timing. They fail because they couldn't withstand the silence. The silence is where the weak give up and the strong evolve.

The Long Road Through Rejection

There comes a point in every founder's journey where the rejection stops feeling like a temporary setback and begins to feel like a verdict. You can only hear no so many times before the echoes start sounding like truth. You can only sit through so many dismissals before the weight begins pressing against your ribs. There were moments in my own path where the silence didn't just frustrate me. It humiliated me. Not in a public, cinematic way, but in a private way that made me question my own internal belief.

I stood in parking lots after meetings that should've gone well, staring at the asphalt as if it held the answer, wondering if I'd misread reality. I drove home from conferences where no one cared what I was building, feeling absurdly small. I watched lesser concepts get traction while mine remained invisible. I sat through dinners with people who nodded politely as if indulging a child, waiting for me to finish explaining something they'd already dismissed in their minds. And each time, a familiar thought crept in: What if they're right? What if I'm wrong? What if this thing I see so clearly is nothing more than the projection of someone desperate to matter? What if the world's silence isn't resistance but a mirror?

This is the psychological hell of the entrepreneurial journey, when you can't tell whether you're being shaped or destroyed. You wake up every day to uncertainty, and the uncertainty becomes a kind of internal erosion. It eats at your confidence. It challenges your identity. It threatens your sense of sanity. Because when the world keeps saying no, the question becomes not "Is the idea good?" but "Am I delusional?" People think entrepreneurs are courageous because of the risks they take, but the real courage is something far different: it's the courage to hold onto a version of reality that only exists in your mind, while everyone around you treats it as fantasy. That level of conviction isn't inspirational. It's brutal. It's lonely. It requires emotional muscles most people never have to use.

I remember one particular season before LARC gained momentum, a stretch of months where every door seemed welded shut. The industry was locked in its ways. Decision makers were comfortable outsourcing the problem rather than solving it. Everyone wanted innovation as long as it didn't require change. I would walk into rooms filled with people who'd spent their entire careers in the same processes, the same assumptions, the same frameworks, and they would listen to me describe a future where packaging wasn't wasteful, wasn't archaic, wasn't fragile, wasn't disposable. But their faces told the truth long before their words did. They weren't ready. Some rejected the idea outright. Others rejected it politely. And the worst were the ones who said, "We love it, but not right now." Those are the rejections that linger, because they disguise they as hope.

What no one tells you is that repeated rejection doesn't just challenge your belief. It challenges your physiology. Your body feels it before your mind can name it. You feel the tightness in your chest after a rough meeting. You feel the collapse in your shoulders walking back to the car. You feel the sting in your gut as you open an email that begins with "unfortunately." You feel the emotional fatigue of trying to appear confident while carrying doubt that threatens to split you open. Founders learn to live inside that discomfort long before they learn how to rise above it.

But inside that pressure, something else begins to form. The pain of rejection gradually transforms from something that weakens you into something that hardens you. You stop expecting validation. You stop waiting for permission. You stop craving applause. You begin to understand that the people telling you no aren't gatekeepers. They're mile markers. Each one reminding you how early you are. Each one silently confirming that the world isn't ready for what you're building, which means you're exactly where you should be. If the world said yes too soon, the idea would be too small.

There's a strange point in this journey where rejection becomes familiar. Not comforting, but recognizable. You begin to expect skepticism. You begin to anticipate doubt. And instead of collapsing under it, you begin to study it. You see patterns in who rejects you and why. You understand that people aren't rejecting your vision. They're protecting their own. They're invested in the world remaining familiar. Your vision threatens that. Your ambition disrupts their comfort. Your clarity exposes their limitations. People don't say no because you're wrong. They say no because you make them confront the possibility that they've stopped growing, stopped imagining, stopped questioning.

One of the hardest lessons I had to learn was that the world doesn't reward originality early. It rewards conformity. It rewards tradition. It rewards safety. And innovators, true innovators, are a threat to all three. This is why the early stage of any revolutionary idea is always marked by a kind of cultural resistance. The world treats the new like a virus. It wants to quarantine it. Test it. Observe it. Wait to see if someone else endorses it first. And until that moment arrives, you exist in a purgatory of potential.

I remember sitting with Chris during those early conversations about LARC, talking about why the industry wasn't moving forward. We saw the same thing: an entire field stuck in the past because it had grown comfortable. Complexity had been accepted instead of challenged. Waste had been normalized instead of solved. Faster, safer, more sustainable, more efficient packaging should've been obvious, but obviousness is irrelevant in a world committed to routine. We realized that the no we kept hearing wasn't about our idea. It was about the world's unwillingness to admit it had been wrong for decades.

This is where founders begin to evolve. They stop interpreting resistance as evidence against their vision and start interpreting it as evidence of how necessary their vision is. The world says no not because it's wise, but because it's slow. It says no because change threatens hierarchies. It says no because people confuse familiarity with correctness. The world's no often has nothing to do with you.

And yet it affects you deeply. It weighs on you. It isolates you. It drains you. You can't pretend otherwise. But as the rejections accumulate, something shifts internally: you start to detach your identity from the world's acceptance. You begin to believe that the silence is survivable. You begin to recognize that your idea has value even when no one sees it. And in that moment, the moment your belief stops depending on external validation, you become dangerous. Not reckless. Not unstable. Dangerous in the sense that the world can no longer move you with its doubt. You stop bending. You stop apologizing. You stop shrinking your vision to fit someone else's comfort. This is the transformation the world never sees: the moment a founder stops seeking approval and starts pursuing inevitability.

Rejection becomes resistance training. Silence becomes the proving ground. Invisibility becomes the fire inside. And the founder becomes the very thing the world has been underestimating. Someone who can't be ignored forever.

The Pressure That Forces Evolution

Every founder eventually reaches a moment when the weight of the world's indifference stops feeling like an obstacle and starts feeling like pressure. Not the kind that crushes you, but the kind that changes your structure. Pressure is one of nature's greatest forces. It turns coal into diamonds, heat into energy, chaos into formation. And in entrepreneurship, rejection becomes a form of pressure so intense that it either snaps you in half or remakes you entirely. The world's no isn't just a word you hear. It's a force that shapes you. It begins gently at first, creeping into the edges of your psyche. You feel it in the fatigue that clings to you after another wasted pitch. You feel it in the way your optimism begins to evaporate halfway through a long day. You feel it in the heaviness that settles in your stomach after you check your inbox, knowing you're about to read another polite dismissal. But then, something begins to happen internally, almost imperceptibly. You start to change.

At first, the change feels like numbness. You stop reacting emotionally to every setback. The rejection doesn't sting the same way. The disappointment loses its sharpness. You begin to expect the no, anticipate it the way a boxer anticipates a punch, and in that anticipation, you stop flinching, recoiling, and collapsing.

You start absorbing. What used to discourage you now strengthens you, because your threshold for pain rises. Your tolerance for uncertainty expands. Your emotional durability grows. You begin to see that the world's rejection can't stop you unless you allow it to define you. And the moment you internalize that truth, you're no longer playing the same game you started in.

The next phase of this transformation is awareness, a new, sharper kind of focus. You begin to recognize patterns in the resistance. You notice that the people who reject you most fiercely are the people most threatened by change. You notice that many of the nos come from individuals who've never built anything themselves. You notice that large organizations are often incapable of understanding early stage innovation because their very structure suffocates imagination. Suddenly, the rejection feels less personal. You stop confusing it with objective truth. Instead, you realize that most people aren't saying no to you. They're saying no to themselves. They're protecting the world they know, even if that world is broken.

And once that awareness takes hold, you begin to adapt, not by shrinking, but by sharpening. You learn to pitch better. You learn to read the room faster. You learn the language of decision makers, the psychology of gatekeepers, the hidden fears of executives who are terrified of being wrong. You learn not to oversell. You learn to let silence work for you. You learn when to push, when to pull back, when to pivot, and when to walk out without flinching. Every rejection becomes data. Every dismissal becomes a lesson. Every "not now" becomes an insight into someone else's limitations.

This is the part of the journey where entrepreneurs develop instincts that can't be taught. You begin to sense opportunity in places where others see failure. You begin to recognize the difference between a genuine barrier and a temporary obstruction. You begin to understand that most closed doors are guarded not by logic, but by fear. And you realize that if you can outlast that fear, even if it takes years, the door eventually opens.

LARC went through this exact evolution. Before we were shipping crates to the largest companies in the world, we were invisible. Before the deals, before the traction, before the inbound calls, there was a long stretch where the idea lived only inside my head. Wood crates had dominated the industry for decades. Innovation had stalled. The industry operated on inertia. And inertia is a powerful enemy. It convinces the world that change is unnecessary.

For years, I heard no, not because the idea was wrong, but because the industry was accustomed to its own blindness. But the pressure of those rejections forced me to get sharper. It forced us to evolve the design, the pitch, the engineering, the pricing, the economics of reuse. Every part of the system became better because the world said no long enough to force us into mastery.

This is the hidden gift of rejection: it compels refinement. Success can make you complacent, but rejection keeps you honest. It forces you to interrogate your assumptions. It forces you to innovate deeper than you would've if the world had accepted your first draft. It forces you to build something that can survive scrutiny, outlast doubt, and withstand real pressure. You don't create excellence in the spotlight. You create it in the dark, when no one is watching, when the world is dismissing you, when your back is pressed against the wall and you have to decide whether you believe in your own vision more than the world does.

The psychological shift that happens here is profound. You stop chasing approval and start chasing inevitability. You stop building to impress and start building to endure. You stop caring if people believe in you because you've finally learned to believe in yourself. And when that happens, rejection no longer threatens you. It becomes irrelevant. The world's no loses its power because you've outgrown the need for its yes.

And then something strange happens. Something almost supernatural in its timing. The world begins to turn. Slowly at first, then all at once. The nos start sounding less certain. The skepticism becomes curiosity. The dismissals turn into questions. People who once ignored you start forwarding your materials to colleagues. Executives who brushed you off begin asking for updates. Companies that rejected you outright suddenly want a second meeting. And when they come back around, they speak as though the idea has just now become obvious to them. They pretend the vision was always clear, as though they saw it from the beginning.

This is the moment entrepreneurs talk about but rarely describe accurately. The turning of the tide. But the tide doesn't turn because the world suddenly becomes wiser. It turns because you didn't quit. You endured the season where no one cared. You pushed through the years when the world doubted you. You refused to disappear in the silence. And because you stayed, the world eventually had no choice but to acknowledge what you'd built.

This is the strange truth about entrepreneurship: the world says no until it can no longer ignore you. The world rejects you until rejecting you becomes stupid. The world doubts you until the evidence becomes impossible to dismiss. The world dismisses you until someone else validates you first. And once the world sees momentum, once it sees customers, revenue, traction, outcomes, it retroactively assigns intelligence to the thing it once treated as foolish. But the real turning point doesn't happen when the world says yes. It happens when the world's no stops mattering. You carry yourself differently. You move differently. You negotiate differently. You operate with the poise of someone who's survived the desert and knows he can survive anything that follows. You no longer question your worth. You no longer debate your vision. You no longer look outside yourself for proof that you're on the right path. The world will eventually say yes, but by the time it does, you won't need it.

And that's the final evolution this chapter moves toward. The moment when the founder realizes that the greatest breakthroughs happen not when the world opens the door, but when you learn to walk through it without waiting for permission in the first place.

Becoming the Founder the World Can No Longer Ignore

The most extraordinary moment in an entrepreneur's journey isn't the one people imagine. It isn't the first big deal or the moment revenue turns into real momentum. It isn't the press write up or the investor interest or the industry finally echoing the language you were using years earlier. Those are meaningful, yes, but they're not the breakthrough. The breakthrough happens long before all that. It happens internally, in a moment so muted you often don't realize it's happened until you look back on it months later. It's the moment when the world's rejection stops changing you. The moment when the no loses its sting. The moment when you stop measuring your worth by someone else's vision. The moment your belief becomes self generated, self sustaining, and self propelled. The moment you realize you no longer need the world to say yes because you already decided that your work is inevitable.

Once you cross that threshold, everything in your psychology shifts. You move differently. You speak differently. You negotiate differently. You stop asking for permission and start outlining your terms. You stop chasing meetings and start choosing them. You stop justifying your existence and start refining your execution. And without announcing it, without forcing it, without posturing or bravado, the world begins treating you differently. People sense when someone has stopped seeking validation. They sense when a founder is no longer fragile. They sense when you're no longer persuading them, but informing them. There's a calmness to it, a steadiness, a subtle power that only comes from someone who's already fought the internal war and won.

It's not ego. It's not arrogance. It's the strength of someone who's survived the dark season and emerged with a spine built in silence. And oddly enough, this is when the world starts saying yes. Not because the world changed, but because you did. You became someone who no longer bends under doubt. You became someone who no longer interprets resistance as failure. You became someone who walks into rooms with the gravity of a person who's built their certainty brick by brick through years of being ignored.

The turning point for LARC didn't come from a single event. It came from accumulation. Thousands of hours refining every edge of the product. Hundreds of conversations that sharpened our understanding of the industry. Countless late nights adjusting designs, improving structural integrity, refining cost models, testing new materials, pushing toward engineering breakthroughs. We didn't suddenly become brilliant. We became more undeniable. And in that undeniability, the tide shifted. One major company leaned in. Then another. Then a third. Suddenly the same executives who'd once dismissed us were reaching out again, and their tone had changed. They spoke with respect. With curiosity. Sometimes even with urgency. But they weren't responding to LARC alone. They were responding to the version of me, of Chris, of our entire team, that had been built in the fires of the years where the world said no.

That's the secret no one writes about: the world doesn't reward the idea. It rewards the evolution of the person behind the idea. You're the product long before the product is. Your psychology becomes the proof of concept. Your endurance becomes the business model. Your resilience becomes the pitch deck. Your certainty becomes the path. Before anyone believes in your company, they'll believe, or disbelieve, in your certainty. That certainty can't be faked. It must be earned. And the only currency that buys it is rejection. The world saying no isn't an obstacle. It's the curriculum.

It teaches you patience when you want speed. It teaches you focus when you want approval. It teaches you self reliance when you want support. It teaches you clarity when you want reassurance. It teaches you conviction when you want comfort. It teaches you leadership before you have followers. It teaches you identity before you have success.

Those lessons accumulate. They reshape your mind. They harden your instincts. They elevate your standards. And they refine your ambition into something cleaner, sharper, and more disciplined than anything you could've crafted in easy seasons.

Once the world's no loses power, something else becomes possible. Something few people ever experience. You stop fearing failure. Not because you believe you won't fail, but because you understand that failure can't dismantle someone who rebuilt themselves from invisibility. When you've gone years without recognition, without reassurance, without external momentum, you learn that you can endure what others can't even imagine. You become anti-fragile. Pressure strengthens you. Doubt clarifies you. Resistance reveals you. You stop looking at obstacles as threats and start seeing them as tests, proof that you're exactly where you should be. And in that state, unshaken, focused, self propelled, you become the kind of founder the world can no longer ignore.

It's at this point that the next stage of the entrepreneurial psyche emerges naturally: the death of ego. Because after you've been broken down, after you've been dismissed, after you've been invisible long enough to learn humility, and after you've become strong enough to no longer crave validation, ego has nothing left to cling to. It fades, not through force, but through irrelevance. And what rises in its place is something far more powerful than bravado. Clarity. The clarity to lead without needing applause. The clarity to take risks without fear of failure. The clarity to make decisions based on mission rather than emotion. The clarity to serve the company instead of leveraging it to serve you.

This is where we go next. To the paradox that confuses most people but defines every great founder's evolution: to build something extraordinary, you must hold both dominance and humility in the same hand. You must carry a vision so massive it borders on arrogance, yet walk with the discipline of someone who knows he's not the center of the story. The mission is.

When the world says no, it tries to break you. But if you survive it, if you embrace it and let the pressure shape you instead of shrink you, you emerge into the next chapter with something unteachable: the internal sovereignty of someone who no longer needs the world's approval to change it.

It sounds like a riddle, and in many ways, it is. But the truth behind this contradiction is simple: the version of you that starts the company is not the version of you capable of leading it to its potential. Something in you must die so something else can grow. That death isn't loud. It isn't dramatic. It isn't an identity crisis or a spiritual awakening or a sudden shift in personality. It's more restrained than that. More internal. It's the gradual surrender of the part of you that needs credit, control, and certainty.

My ego took its deepest wounds long before LARC ever existed. Years of rejection stripped it. Years of being underestimated pierced it. Years of wandering through periods where the world didn't believe in me forced it to shrink. But the most powerful blows came from the moments I failed publicly, misjudged privately, or pushed too hard in the wrong direction. In those moments, ego wasn't a shield. It was a blindfold. It made me defensive when I needed to be curious. It made me stubborn when I needed to pivot. It made me hold too tightly to ideas that needed to die so better ones could emerge. Ego makes you reactive when you should be strategic. It makes you territorial when you should be collaborative. It makes you fragile when you desperately need to be flexible.

And yet I also know the other side of that truth: without ego, I never would've survived the early years. I never would've stepped into the battlefield at all. I never would've built the first prototype, pitched the first idea, endured the first rejection, or taken the risks that cost me sleep, money, relationships, and peace. Ego isn't the enemy. Ego is the starter engine. It's what gets you onto the field, onto the battlefield, into the fire. It gives you permission to believe when no one else does. It insulates you from doubt long enough to build momentum. But once the mission grows larger than you, ego must get smaller.

I watched this play out firsthand as LARC evolved. When Chris came in, when our team started forming, when real talent began surrounding the vision, I had to confront a truth no founder enjoys confronting: I couldn't do this alone. And more importantly, I wasn't supposed to. The company needed minds sharper than mine in specific areas. It needed operators who saw angles I missed, engineers who could build beyond my technical limits, strategists who could analyze what I felt, and people who could turn the raw fire inside me into structured execution.

Leadership isn't about being the smartest in the room. It's about building a room filled with people who surpass you in all the places you're weak. Ego hates that truth. Vision loves it. Mission requires it.

"When I let go of what I am,
I become what I might be."

- Lao Tzu

8

The Death of Ego

The Paradox at the Center of Every Founder

Every entrepreneur eventually reaches a moment where their greatest enemy is no longer the market, the competition, the capital, the timing, the uncertainty, or even the world's rejection. At a certain point, the external war becomes still enough for you to hear the real one, the one inside your own head. And it becomes inescapably clear that the biggest threat to your mission isn't what stands in front of you, but what stands within you. This is the moment when ego enters the arena. Not the cartoon version of ego that people throw around casually, but the deeper, more insidious ego that masquerades as confidence, disguises itself as conviction, and whispers to you in the exact same tone as your intuition. Ego is clever like that. It never introduces itself. It never says, "I'm here to sabotage you." It arrives wearing your face.

You need a certain amount of ego to start a company in the first place. There's no way around that truth. You must believe, at some level, that you're capable of building something others can't. You must believe that you can see what others overlook, that you can endure what others avoid, that you can hold a vision larger than anything your past has prepared you for. You must believe that you can take a blank page and turn it into a living, breathing entity that influences the world. That belief requires ego. Not arrogance. Ego. A healthy, sturdy sense of self that doesn't crumble at the first sign of doubt.

But the moment you begin to grow, the moment your idea becomes a company and your company becomes a mission, that same ego becomes a liability. It becomes friction. It becomes noise. It becomes the very thing that'll blind you to threats, distort your decisions, and convince you that you're the reason for the success rather than the steward of it. Ego is both the spark and the smoke. It's the ignition that starts the engine and the haze that can eventually choke it out.

You can't build anything meaningful without ego. And you can't scale anything meaningful with it. This is the paradox no one warns founders about. People tell you to be confident, but not too confident. Bold, but not reckless. Visionary, but grounded. Assertive, but humble.

It sounds like a riddle, and in many ways, it is. But the truth behind this contradiction is simple: the version of you that starts the company isn't the version of you capable of leading it to its potential. Something in you must die so something else can grow. That death isn't loud. It isn't dramatic. It isn't an identity crisis or a spiritual awakening or a sudden shift in personality. It's more subtle than that. More internal. It's the gradual surrender of the part of you that needs credit, control, and certainty.

My ego took its deepest wounds long before LARC ever existed. Years of rejection stripped it. Years of being underestimated pierced it. Years of wandering through periods where the world didn't believe in me forced it to shrink. But the most powerful blows came from the moments I failed publicly, misjudged privately, or pushed too hard in the wrong direction. In those moments, ego wasn't a shield. It was a blindfold. It made me defensive when I needed to be curious. It made me stubborn when I needed to pivot. It made me hold too tightly to ideas that needed to die so better ones could emerge. Ego makes you reactive when you should be strategic. It makes you territorial when you should be collaborative. It makes you fragile when you desperately need to be flexible.

And yet I also know the other side of that truth: without ego, I never would've survived the early years. I never would've stepped into the battlefield at all. I never would've built the first prototype, pitched the first idea, endured the first rejection, or taken the risks that cost me sleep, money, relationships, and peace. Ego isn't the enemy. Ego is the starter engine. It's what gets you onto the field, onto the battlefield, into the fire. It gives you permission to believe when no one else does. It insulates you from doubt long enough to build momentum. But once the mission grows larger than you, ego must get smaller.

I watched this evolution firsthand as LARC expanded. When talented people started surrounding the vision, I had to confront a truth no founder enjoys confronting: I couldn't do this alone. And more importantly, I wasn't supposed to. The company needed minds sharper than mine in specific areas. It needed operators who saw angles I missed, engineers who could build beyond my technical limits, strategists who could analyze what I felt, and people who could turn the raw fire inside me into structured execution.

Leadership isn't about being the smartest in the room. It's about building a room filled with people who surpass you in all the places you're weak. Ego hates that truth. Vision loves it. Mission requires it.

The Shedding of the Self That Cannot Lead You Forward

Ego doesn't die in a single dramatic moment. It erodes slowly, through experience, through failure, through friction, through the humiliation of being wrong in front of people you respect, and through the repeated realization that the company you're building has ambitions that exceed your personal limits. Ego death isn't poetic. It isn't glamorous. It isn't the enlightened awakening that motivational books pretend it is. It feels more like being scraped from the inside, like shedding a layer of skin you didn't realize you'd been wearing for years. And because of that, most founders resist it far longer than they should.

The first stage of ego death often begins with friction, the internal kind. When you find yourself clinging to ideas that no longer make sense, insisting on your own correctness long after evidence suggests otherwise, or fighting your team instead of listening to them, you're not defending the mission. You're defending the fragile parts of your identity. I remember moments early in LARC's development where I pushed too hard in the wrong direction simply because I'd convinced myself that my original thinking was untouchable. Being the founder makes it dangerously easy to assume your instincts are always right. But instincts, like everything else, must evolve. When exceptional talent arrived, it brought clarity that exposed the parts of my thinking that needed refinement, structure, or complete overhaul. And in those moments, I felt that small sting of defensiveness, the protest of ego saying, "Don't let go. Don't admit you need help."

That reaction is human. But if you let it govern you, it becomes the beginning of your downfall. Ego convinces you that you must have all the answers. Leadership teaches you that you shouldn't. The first real shedding happens when you stop fighting the people who are trying to elevate the mission, and you start appreciating how their strengths illuminate your blind spots. The moment you can look at another person's brilliance and feel gratitude instead of insecurity, you've taken your first step into real leadership.

The second stage of ego death emerges through failure. Small, failures that expose the cracks in your thinking. The deals you lose because you underestimated the customer. The moments where you overpromised because you thought enthusiasm was a strategy. The times you were so certain you didn't ask enough questions. The situations where your impatience cost you time, money, or trust. These failures don't attack your company.

They attack your self image. Failure strips away illusions. It pulls your ego out of your hands one finger at a time. And if you allow it to, failure teaches you a language that ego can't speak: humility grounded in reality.

I learned this the hard way. There were times when I believed I could outwork any gap. When I thought intensity alone was enough to compensate for structure. When I relied on instinct instead of preparation. When I assumed my conviction was enough to convince the world. But the world doesn't move because you want it to. It moves because you adapt to it. Every time I hit a wall, whether emotional, operational, or strategic, I had to confront a truth that ego despises: wanting to be right isn't nearly as valuable as becoming effective. Ego cares about being correct. Leadership cares about being better. The two are rarely aligned.

The losses I accumulated weren't failures. They were data. Every rejected deal revealed a gap in my positioning. Every skeptical customer exposed an assumption I'd held too loosely. Every misstep showed me where precision mattered more than passion. I didn't learn humility through defeat. I learned leverage through feedback. The difference is crucial. Ego interprets correction as attack. Intelligence interprets correction as optimization. I chose optimization. Not because I was humble, but because I was ruthless about improving the mission. Weakness would've been refusing to evolve. Strength was weaponizing every lesson.

The third stage of ego death reveals itself in team dynamics. When you begin building something bigger than yourself, you realize rapidly that people don't follow founders. They follow missions. They follow integrity. They follow leaders who know who they are and must also know who they aren't.

The death of ego demands that you stop measuring your value by how essential you are and start measuring it by how empowered your people become. The shift is subtle but absolute: instead of trying to be the smartest in the room, you become the one who creates space for the smartest in the room to thrive.

I've watched talented founders choke their own companies because their ego refused to make room for others. They needed the spotlight, the credit, the control. They couldn't handle the discomfort of someone else being better than them at something fundamental to the business. But in real innovation, that discomfort isn't a threat. It's the curriculum.

If you're the strongest at everything, the company will remain small enough to be carried by one person. If you surround yourself with people who surpass you, your company grows beyond what one person could ever hold.

The turning point came when I stopped viewing exceptional talent as competition and started seeing it as multiplication. When people arrived whose strengths exposed my limitations, I had a choice: defend my territory or expand the mission. The engineering precision, the operational discipline, the methodical approach to complex systems that others brought, these weren't threats. They were force multipliers. The moment I realized that their talents strengthened the mission more than they threatened my identity was the moment the company began to accelerate. That was only possible because ego loosened its grip.

The fourth stage of ego death comes from the weight of responsibility. As your company grows, your decisions begin to affect real people. Their careers. Their families. Their time. Their trust. There's a sobering reality that emerges when you realize that leadership isn't about being celebrated. It's about being accountable. Ego wants admiration. Leadership accepts consequence. When you lead a team, you can't hide behind ego. You can't shield yourself from the cost of your decisions. You stand in front of the mission, not to be applauded, but to take the hit first.

This responsibility reshapes you. It forces maturity. It reveals the difference between wanting authority and earning authority. And as those stakes rise, ego naturally begins to lose relevance. You no longer make decisions to satisfy your pride. You make them to protect the mission and the people carrying it forward.

The death of ego isn't a full disappearance of the self. It's the extraction of everything that weakens your ability to lead. What remains afterward is clarity. The clarity to adapt instead of defend. To trust your team instead of fear their talent. To say "I don't know" without shame. To ask for help. To remove your ego from the center of the mission and replace it with purpose.

As the founder evolves, ego becomes unneeded. Not eliminated, but irrelevant. And that irrelevance is a kind of freedom. You're no longer defending an identity. You're building a future.

The Leader Who Emerges When Ego Finally Lets Go

The most powerful evolution in a founder's psychology happens the moment they stop building a company to prove something and start building it because the mission demands it. This shift is subtle to the outside world, almost invisible, but internally it changes the very structure of how you move. Ego builds for recognition. Leadership builds for impact. Ego craves acknowledgment. Leadership craves execution. Ego wants to be seen as the architect. Leadership wants the architecture to stand on its own.

And there's a point, a necessary one, where the founder realizes that the company no longer needs the version of them who started it. It needs the version who can expand it without needing to be the central hero.

This realization rarely arrives in triumphant fashion. It arrives in moments of pressure, the kind that strip away performance and force you into truth. You begin to feel the weight of the mission differently. Not as a platform for your identity, but as something entrusted to you, something that'll outlast you if you steward it correctly.

With LARC, that moment came as the company began gaining real traction. Major customers. Complex engineering demands. A rapidly expanding team. The mission was suddenly too big to be held by one person's ego. It required collaboration at a level deeper than pride ever allows. It required precision that couldn't be faked. It required a willingness to let others carry the mission forward in ways only they could. And it required the discipline to step back when stepping forward no longer served the company.

A founder who's truly shed ego stops needing to be the smartest in the room and instead works to assemble a room filled with minds that surpass his own. He stops protecting his position and starts protecting the mission. He stops asking "What do I need to prove?" and starts asking "What does the company need to become?"

The shift is internal but the results are structural. Decisions get faster because you're not filtering them through pride. Talent gets stronger because you're not threatened by excellence. Strategy gets clearer because you're not bending it to accommodate your need for control. What emerges is a leader built not on certainty, but on capacity. Not on dominance, but on discernment. Not on being irreplaceable, but on making yourself unnecessary.

Watching the people around me grow into their roles forced a profound truth to the surface. Chris brought engineering mastery that turned abstract vision into structural precision. Others developed systems I never could've built. The team executed with a level of detail that pushed the mission beyond what any single person could carry. The more exceptional your team becomes, the more unnecessary ego feels. When you see brilliance around you, the impulse to cling to your own authority naturally fades. You want to give them the space they deserve. You want the mission to be fueled by collective strength, not constrained by the founder's insecurities.

The most profound transformation happens in the relationship between the founder and the mission. When ego dies, the mission becomes the dominant force. It becomes the priority above pride, above convenience, above personal comfort. At that point, you no longer lead the mission. The mission leads you.

It becomes the standard by which decisions are measured. It becomes the compass when uncertainty hits. It becomes the anchor when doubt creeps in. And when the mission becomes that powerful, ego simply doesn't have a place anymore. It can't coexist with a purpose that demands clarity, precision, and discipline.

This evolution also reveals a deeper truth: ego is loud, but purpose is quiet. Ego needs an audience. Purpose needs action. Ego exhausts you. Purpose steadies you. Ego inflates. Purpose grounds. And once you've experienced the grounding effect of purpose, ego begins to feel like noise, a distraction you no longer have the patience for. You move differently because you're being pulled by something larger than recognition, something that doesn't require applause to justify its existence, something that exists whether you're celebrated or invisible, something that continues long after your name fades from memory.

Finally, the death of ego produces a kind of leadership that's both rare and unmistakable: the leader who can walk into a room without needing to dominate it. The leader who can hand power to others without feeling lesser. The leader who can give credit away freely, accept blame without flinching, and make decisions that may never earn applause but will strengthen the company. The leader who understands that their legacy isn't their name, but the stability and strength of what they built. The leader who knows that the only hierarchy that truly matters is the hierarchy of competence, and that the mission itself is the highest authority. This is the leader who emerges when ego finally lets go, the one capable of scaling a mission beyond the limits of any individual, including the founder who first imagined it.

The Identity That Remains Once Ego Is Gone

The final stage of ego death isn't a moment. It's an identity. It's a way of existing, one that emerges only after you've been stripped down to something essential, something clear, something that no longer needs validation, control, or applause to move forward. When ego finally lets go, what remains is a version of yourself that the world can't manipulate, can't rattle, can't inflate, and can't diminish. You become steady. Grounded in a way that has nothing to do with arrogance and everything to do with alignment.

This version of you no longer enters a room thinking, "How do I prove myself?" You enter thinking, "How do I serve the mission?" You no longer fear being wrong because you're no longer building your identity on the illusion of being right. Being wrong becomes a tool, a directional correction toward becoming better, sharper, more effective. Decisions stop being about pride and start being about precision. Meetings stop being about authority and start being about clarity. Leadership stops being about visibility and starts being about responsibility. And the company stops being a reflection of your ego and becomes a reflection of your discipline. At this stage, something powerful happens to your relationship with success.

When ego is alive, success becomes addictive. It makes you chase the spotlight. It feeds the urge to be recognized, admired, validated. But once ego dies, success becomes secondary. Not unimportant, just demoted. It becomes the outcome, not the obsession. The mission becomes the obsession. The work becomes the reward. The execution becomes the satisfaction. You no longer measure success by how much the world sees. You measure it by how deeply the company is aligned with its purpose, how effectively the team executes, how consistently the vision is translated into reality. Success becomes something you steward, not something you chase.

This shift makes you more resilient. When ego is in control, failure feels like annihilation. It threatens your identity. But when ego has died, failure becomes information. It becomes feedback. It becomes a recalibration tool. You don't crumble when things go wrong. You adjust. You don't spiral when plans fall apart. You reframe. You don't panic when the unexpected hits. You anchor yourself in purpose and move forward. Without ego, failure no longer wounds you. It shapes you.

This is also where leadership gains real potency. When a founder sheds ego, the team senses it immediately. They feel safer speaking truth. They trust that disagreement won't be punished. They invest themselves more deeply because they know the mission isn't built on the fragile foundation of one person's pride. A company led by a founder who's killed their ego becomes a place where competence thrives, where ideas rise from every corner, where people feel ownership because the mission feels shared, not possessed. And when people feel ownership, they pour their strength, their creativity, their ingenuity, and their devotion into the work. They become coauthors of the mission instead of spectators in someone else's story.

This is exactly why some companies scale and others crumble. The companies that crumble are led by founders who can't release control, can't accept feedback, can't empower others, can't see past their own reflection. The companies that scale are led by founders who understand that leadership isn't about being the hero. It's about building a system where heroes can emerge everywhere. Ego demands centrality. Leadership demands distribution.

The companies that scale are led by founders who understand that leadership isn't about being the hero. It's about building a system where heroes can emerge everywhere. Ego demands centrality. Leadership demands distribution. Ego dominates. Leadership elevates.

As LARC matured, I saw this firsthand. I saw what happened when I stepped back enough for others to step forward. I saw what happened when I stopped trying to be the force behind every movement and became the architect of the environment instead. The company began to grow not through me, but through us. Through the engineers. Through the operators. Through the strategists. Through the people who brought their talents to bear in ways that weren't just equal to mine, but often far superior. And this wasn't a threat. It was a relief. It meant the mission had grown beyond me. It meant the company could survive without being tethered to my personal limitations. It meant the vision had become large enough to require many hands, and strong enough to hold them.

The death of ego is ultimately the birth of longevity. Because once the founder steps out of the spotlight and into the true role of guardian, strategist, and steward, the company gains the one thing ego can never provide: durability. A company attached to a founder's ego dies when the founder falters. A company detached from ego survives because it's built on systems, principles, talent, and mission, not personality.

When ego dies, leadership deepens. When leadership deepens, legacy begins.

And legacy isn't about being remembered. It's about what remains standing long after you're gone. It's about the culture you create, the people you empower, the systems you build, and the mission you imprint so deeply into the DNA of the company that it keeps moving even after you step aside. Legacy isn't ego. Legacy is stewardship. Legacy is discipline. Legacy is clarity. Legacy is the imprint of a leader who learned to stand aside so the mission could stand on its own.

When ego is gone, you no longer feel the need to be at the center of the story. You feel the need to make sure the story continues. And in that realization, quiet, clear, and steady, you become the leader the mission always required.

When ego is alive, success becomes addictive. It makes you chase the spotlight. It feeds the urge to be recognized, admired, validated. But once ego dies, success becomes secondary. Not unimportant, just demoted.

It becomes the outcome, not the obsession. The mission becomes the obsession. The work becomes the reward. The execution becomes the satisfaction. You no longer measure success by how much the world sees. You measure it by how deeply the company is aligned with its purpose, how effectively the team executes, how consistently the vision is translated into reality. Success becomes something you steward, not something you chase.

This shift makes you more resilient. When ego is in control, failure feels like annihilation. It threatens your identity. But when ego has died, failure becomes information. It becomes feedback. It becomes a recalibration tool. You don't crumble when things go wrong. You adjust. You don't spiral when plans fall apart. You reframe. You don't panic when the unexpected hits. You anchor yourself in purpose and move forward. Without ego, failure no longer wounds you. It shapes you. And this is also where leadership gains real potency. When a founder sheds ego, the team senses it immediately. They feel safer speaking truth. They trust that disagreement won't be punished. They invest themselves more deeply because they know the mission isn't built on the fragile foundation of one person's pride. A company led by a founder who's killed their ego becomes a place where competence thrives, where ideas rise from every corner, where people feel ownership because the mission feels shared, not possessed.

But resilience without staying power is just survival. Leadership without stamina is just performance. The death of ego clears the way, but it doesn't guarantee you'll last. Because what comes next isn't a question of vision or clarity or even purpose. It's a question of endurance. The ability to keep moving when momentum dies. The capacity to hold the line when every signal tells you to quit. The strength to push through years, not weeks, of building. And endurance is where most founders fail, not because they lack talent, but because they run out of fuel long before the mission runs its course.

"Fall seven times, stand up eight."

- Japanese Proverb

9

The Art of Endurance

The Seasons Few Survive

Entrepreneurship isn't won by talent, intelligence, luck, or even great ideas. It's won by endurance, the slow, excruciating, invisible art of continuing long after every rational signal tells you to stop. There comes a point in every founder's journey when momentum evaporates, when the world stops paying attention, when the early believers go quiet, when capital stalls, when customers hesitate, when nothing seems to move despite every ounce of force you apply. These seasons aren't the exception. They're the rule. They're the crucible through which every real builder must pass, and they've broken more would be entrepreneurs than bad ideas ever did. The public sees the sprint. The private truth is the marathon.

Endurance isn't glamorous. It isn't exciting. It isn't inspiring in the moment. It feels like slogging through mud while the world races ahead on pavement. It feels like pushing a boulder uphill while everyone else seems to glide. It feels like waking up every morning to the same problems that refused to budge the day before, and forcing yourself to face them again with the same intensity, the same discipline, the same stubborn refusal to give up. Endurance begins where motivation dies. It begins after inspiration fades and long before results return. And that's precisely why so few people ever develop it.

The truth is, most people quit too early not because they're weak, but because the human psyche isn't designed for extended periods of uncertainty. We're wired for feedback loops, for reward cycles, for some sign that our effort is producing progress. But entrepreneurship denies you all of that for long stretches of time. It's a psychological desert. The early excitement evaporates. The novelty disappears. The promises you made to yourself start to feel hollow. You begin to wonder if you miscalculated everything. And even worse, there are no witnesses. There's no applause. No validation. No reassurance. No one telling you that you're close. You must learn to generate certainty from a place where none exists. That's the art of endurance.

When I look back on the evolution of LARC, I can see the endurance cycles clearly. There were long months when doors closed faster than we could knock on them. Times when customers said all the right things but never followed through. Times when we were building crates in the shadows, bootstrapping, hustling, scraping together resources, trying to convince an industry to believe in something that didn't exist yet. Times when the burn rate hovered too close to the edge. Times when every decision carried weight. Times when we were one stroke of bad luck away from collapse. People imagine that companies turn on a single moment of breakthrough. The truth is that they turn on a thousand moments of not quitting.

The world today glamorizes grit, but it rarely talks about what grit actually feels like. Grit isn't motivational posters or inspirational speeches. Grit is grinding through a Tuesday afternoon with no progress in sight. Grit is answering emails you don't want to answer. Grit is taking calls that drain you. Grit is rebuilding pitch decks at midnight. Grit is carrying a company on your back through stretches of total silence from the world. Grit is riding out drought cycles that would make most people collapse. Grit is doing the work with no guarantee that the work will be enough.

People see entrepreneurs as visionaries, but vision means nothing without endurance. Vision is the spark. Endurance is the oxygen. One without the other dies quickly.

In the early days, there were moments at LARC when the only thing keeping the mission alive was the sheer force of belief. Belief in the idea. Belief in the necessity of what we were building. Belief in the future we knew existed even when no one else could see it. Belief in the people beside us. Belief in the quiet promise we made to ourselves on the worst days of our lives: that we wouldn't go back to the person we were before this began.

Endurance isn't about the grind. It's about identity. You endure because quitting would violate who you are at the core. You endure because you've wrestled with yourself enough times to know that the discomfort of persistence is nothing compared to the devastation of abandoning your potential. You endure because once you've glimpsed the life you could build, the life you're currently living becomes too small to tolerate.

This is where many entrepreneurs miss the mark. They confuse discomfort with a sign to stop. They interpret resistance as misalignment. They look for ease as proof they're on the right path. But the right path is rarely the easiest one. In fact, the right path often reveals itself precisely because of its difficulty. The resistance is the signal. The obstacles are the markers. The struggle is the confirmation that you're not playing small.

Chris and I saw this pattern repeat itself over and over, not just in the company's growth, but in ourselves. There were days when we both wondered how much more weight we could carry. There were moments when we felt like the entire mission was resting on a thread. There were late nights, early mornings, and stretches so mentally exhausting that the body simply followed along out of habit because the mind was too tired to lead. But every time we pushed through, something shifted quietly. A crack opened. A small win appeared. A new opportunity surfaced. The boulder moved an inch. And in the world of endurance, an inch is enough to keep going. The entrepreneur who survives isn't the one who avoids the drought. It's the one who continues through it.

This is the core principle behind the psychological endurance required for anything meaningful: nothing changes until you refuse to give up. It may take months. It may take years. It may take longer than your patience, your savings, or your sanity would prefer. But the breakthrough, the real breakthrough, arrives only after you've outlasted everything designed to make you quit.

And that brings us to the next truth, the one rarely spoken aloud: endurance is lonely. Even when you have a team. Even when you have partners. Even when you have support. The weight is still yours. The responsibility is still yours. The vision is still yours. The consequences are still yours. There's an internal solitude to being the founder that nothing can fully soften. It's not a flaw. It's the nature of the role. You carry the torch, and if the flame dies, you don't get to blame the wind. But loneliness isn't the enemy. Loneliness is the path.

In the next section, we'll explore exactly how that solitude shapes the founder's psychology, how endurance becomes a spiritual discipline, and why the entrepreneur who learns to stay when the world goes silent becomes unstoppable.

The Three Year Rule

Every meaningful company has a three year season that determines its fate. It's not always the first three years, and it rarely aligns cleanly with financial milestones, but every founder eventually enters a stretch of roughly thirty six months where everything matters and nothing works. It's the period when you must build faster than the world believes in you, when you must sell a vision long before you have the product maturity to justify it, when you must lead people through uncertainty without the validation that their efforts will pay off. It's the window which the company either becomes real or becomes memory.

Most great businesses look inevitable in hindsight, but in the moment they were built, they looked impossible. Amazon looked like a bookstore that couldn't make money. Tesla looked like a vanity project for a wealthy eccentric. SpaceX looked like a suicide mission. Airbnb looked like a bizarre hobby. I could list ten thousand more. Every enduring company goes through the same pattern: the three year rule. A stretch of relentless effort during which almost nothing scales, capital comes slowly, the product evolves painfully, customers require convincing, and the founder must push harder than seems rational.

LARC had its own three year crucible. There were long periods where it felt like a tug of war against gravity itself. We were proving a category, not just a product. We were asking trillion dollar industries to abandon a century old model. We were entering a domain where the status quo was so entrenched it bordered on religious. Wooden crates had existed since ancient Egypt. And we were saying, "This is done. There's a better way. The future won't be built on wood." That kind of message isn't welcomed. It's resisted, dismissed, even mocked. But the three year rule rewards those who outlast resistance.

It was during this stretch that the team cemented into something extraordinary. It was during this period that I watched Chris carry engineering challenges with a level of calm that allowed us to take on impossible timelines. It was during this period that Kate's steady presence kept me from imploding under the weight of expectation. It was during this period that faith, the deep, personal, spiritual kind, became a necessity rather than a comfort. When everything external feels fragile, the internal must become unbreakable.

Every founder I've met who built something of true significance went through their own thirty six month crucible. They all share the same scars. They all tell the same story in different words: "It should've died, but I refused to let it." That refusal isn't stubbornness. It's survival instinct. And the founder who develops it becomes immune to circumstances. They stop asking, "Is this possible?" and start asking, "What must be done next?" They shift from emotional decision making to strategic adaptation. They transcend the psychological noise that destroys most people long before external failure ever does.

This is the moment where endurance proves itself to be the most underrated competitive advantage in entrepreneurship. The founder who's willing to suffer longer, persist longer, adjust longer, and hold the vision longer will outpace those who rely on talent alone. Talent is a spark. Endurance is the path. Talent gets you in the room. Endurance stays there until the work is complete.

This three year stretch teaches a final, humbling lesson: nothing meaningful is ever built as fast as you want it to be. And that's intentional. The slow pace forces you to mature alongside the company. If the results arrived too quickly, you wouldn't be ready to hold them. If success landed before you'd developed the internal musculature to sustain it, it would collapse under your weight. Endurance stretches you into the version of yourself capable of carrying the future you're building.

By the time you emerge from the three year crucible, you're no longer the person who entered it. You've been reshaped by pressure, by patience, by discipline, by the grind, and by the psychological war that only founders can understand. You become sharper. Calmer. More strategic. More dangerous. More unshakable. More certain. And the company reflects that transformation. This is the art of endurance: the understanding that the seasons of silence aren't punishment. They're preparation.

When Endurance Becomes Identity

The moment you realize that you can withstand anything is the moment the world loses its power to break you. It happens quietly. You wake up one morning after years of grinding and realize that you no longer fear the drought cycles. You no longer panic when the path disappears. You no longer question whether you have what it takes. You've endured enough storms to know you can outlast the next one. You've failed enough times to trust your ability to recover. You've carried enough weight to be confident that nothing can truly crush you now.

It's a shift in the way you breathe, the way you move, the way you lead, the way you think. Problems that once destabilized you now feel manageable. Setbacks that once felt catastrophic now feel temporary. Doubt that once whispered loudly now loses its voice. Endurance becomes your operating system.

And something else happens, equally powerful: the team feels it. When the founder becomes steady, the culture becomes steady. When the founder becomes resilient, the company becomes resilient. When the founder becomes a source of calm pressure, the organization learns to execute under stress. The founder sets the emotional temperature of the enterprise, and when that temperature is anchored in endurance rather than anxiety, the company scales from a place of strength.

This is the stage where vision expands naturally. You're no longer fighting for survival. You're building for legacy. You begin to think beyond quarters and years and start thinking in decades. You begin to see opportunities others miss because you've trained yourself to live beyond the noise, beyond the urgency, beyond the immediate. You become a long term architect in a short term world.

By the end of this transformation, endurance is no longer something you practice. It's something you are. And when endurance becomes identity, nothing can stop you, not because the journey gets easier, but because you do.

This marks the pivot into the next evolution: the war with the self. After endurance has shaped you, there remains one last enemy, the internal saboteur, the psychological residue of your past, the old patterns that rise just when you're on the edge of breakthrough.

And that battle becomes the next test.

"The first and greatest victory is to conquer yourself."

- Plato

10

The War With Yourself

The Enemy Within the Walls

Every founder eventually discovers that the greatest danger to their mission isn't competition, market timing, supply chain constraints, capital droughts, or technological challenges. The greatest danger is themselves. Not the self they show the world, the competent self, the confident self, the strategic self, but the self that lives behind the eyes, the self shaped by old wounds, old fears, old patterns, old narratives, and old emotional coding that developed long before the company ever existed. This is the enemy within the walls. And no one escapes this part of the journey.

The war with yourself begins beneath the surface. It doesn't arrive with a sword drawn. It arrives with hesitation, with small doubts, with the soft whisper that you're not enough, with the subtle pull back toward safety. It arrives in the form of questions you thought you outgrew, insecurities you thought you buried, and memories you believed you'd left behind. You think you're building a company, but you're really excavating parts of yourself that have been waiting beneath the surface for years, sometimes decades. You think the resistance is external, but the external resistance only becomes a mirror for the internal battle you've avoided confronting.

This is the stage of entrepreneurship where the stakes shift from financial to psychological. You begin to realize that the company will only grow as far as you grow. That no amount of strategy can compensate for an unresolved internal conflict. That the business can't transcend the limitations you refuse to face. It's a humbling realization, the kind that strips away ego, bravado, and the illusion of control. You're forced to look inward, not because you want to, but because the company demands it.

LARC pushed me into this war with ruthless precision. As the stakes grew, the pressure uncovered vulnerabilities I thought time had sealed shut. The emotional scars from earlier chapters of my life, the instability of childhood, the turbulence of young adulthood, the battles with authority, the rage of being misunderstood, the wounds from betrayal, resurfaced under the weight of leadership. Not dramatically. Not all at once. But through small reactions that didn't belong to the present moment. A flinch of doubt when certainty was required. A flash of anger when patience would've served better. A tightening of control when delegation was the wiser path. A surge of intensity when the team needed calm. These weren't business reactions. They were personal echoes. The war with yourself is never about the moment you're in. It's about the moments you never resolved.

Every founder brings ghosts into the company, ghosts of fear, ghosts of inadequacy, ghosts of unresolved loss, ghosts of anger, ghosts of abandonment. They show up in disguised forms. The fear of being wrong becomes micromanagement. The fear of being judged becomes avoidance. The fear of losing control becomes rigidity. The fear of being hurt becomes emotional distance. The fear of being powerless becomes aggression. The fear of failure becomes self sabotage. And if left unchecked, these ghosts begin to run the company more than you do.

The world loves to talk about founder burnout as if it's merely the result of long hours and high pressure. But burnout isn't exhaustion. Burnout is identity conflict. Burnout happens when the person you are internally is fighting the person the mission requires you to be. Burnout happens when the company's evolution outpaces your own. Burnout happens when you cling to old emotional patterns that are incompatible with the scale of the vision in front of you. Burnout isn't the fire going out. Burnout is the fire consuming the structure that contains it.

The war with yourself intensifies when success begins to appear on the horizon. This is the part no one warns you about. You think the internal struggle will end once the company gains momentum. You imagine that validation will quiet the doubt, that traction will silence the old fears, that progress will resolve the old injuries. But success doesn't erase internal battles. It magnifies them. Success raises the stakes. Success exposes the cracks. Success forces you to level up emotionally at the same speed you level up operationally, financially, strategically. If you don't grow, the company will outgrow you. And that's where the real war begins.

There were moments, especially in the early scaling phases of LARC, when I realized the greatest threat to the mission wasn't external at all, it was me. Not because I lacked intelligence or creativity or discipline, but because I still carried internal patterns that didn't belong in the arena I was entering. My anger, which had once protected me, needed refinement. My intensity, which had once driven me, needed direction. My distrust, which had once kept me safe, needed calibration. My independence, which had once allowed me to survive, needed to evolve into interdependence. And perhaps most importantly, my belief that I had to carry everything alone needed to die.

This realization doesn't come gently. It breaks you open. You discover that survival mode wiring, while valuable in the early scrappy phase, becomes destructive in the scaling phase. The traits that kept you alive become the traits that can kill the company. The walls you built for protection become the walls that block the next level. And you face the uncomfortable truth that the next evolution of the business requires the next evolution of you.

This is the moment every founder resists, the moment where you must confront the part of yourself that's still shaped by fear. Fear of losing control. Fear of being seen. Fear of vulnerability. Fear of failure. Fear of success. Fear of stepping into a version of yourself you haven't yet learned how to inhabit. But the company can't wait for your comfort. It demands your transformation. It requires the death of the old self so the new one can lead. The war with yourself isn't about choosing victory. It's about choosing transformation. And transformation is violent in its honesty.

The next sections will explore how this war intensifies, how sabotage begins to hunt you the moment you're closest to breakthrough, and how the founder must learn to dismantle the internal enemy piece by piece, until what remains is a version of themselves capable of carrying the future they're building.

The Battle You Can't Outsource

The internal war intensifies in the quiet hours, when no one's watching, when the emails stop, when the calls end, when the office goes still, and the weight of the day settles. It's here, in the moments without motion, that the old self begins to fight back. The self built from fear. The self built from childhood defense mechanisms. The self built from the wounds that first taught you to armor up. The self built from the lessons forged in pain before you ever knew what pain could cost you.

Entrepreneurs rarely admit it, but the scariest part of building a company isn't the market, not the customers, not the competitors, it's the realization that you're capable of undermining everything you've built. You feel this the first time you hesitate on a decision you know you should make. You feel it the first time you avoid a hard conversation. You feel it when you shrink from a moment that demands expansion. You feel it when you procrastinate on something crucial not because you're lazy, but because you're afraid of what happens if you execute it perfectly.

Sabotage isn't a defect. It's a leftover survival instinct. A misguided protector. A psychological bodyguard who doesn't understand that you no longer live in the environment that created it.

When I first felt LARC reaching its next stage, the stage where the world was beginning to understand what we were building, something unexpected happened inside me. A familiar voice resurfaced, one I hadn't heard since the darkest years of my life. It whispered old stories. Stories about staying small. Stories about not trusting anyone. Stories about bracing for betrayal even when no betrayal was present. Stories about not letting success in too far because success, in my past, had always been followed by loss.

This is the enemy founders face: your nervous system knows your past better than your future, and it's designed to bring you back to the last place it felt safe. Even if that place was misery. Even if that place was smallness. It doesn't matter how skilled you are. It doesn't matter how disciplined you are. It doesn't matter how intelligent or visionary you are. If the old emotional patterns still control the operating system, they'll eventually take the wheel.

This is why so many brilliant founders collapse just before the breakthrough. It's not because they lacked capacity. It's because the future they were walking into required a version of themselves they hadn't yet learned to become. And instead of transforming, they defaulted to the identity built in the earlier, smaller chapters of their lives. The internal enemy whispers different things to different people. To me, it whispered intensity without direction. It whispered distrust when I needed connection. It whispered independence when I needed interdependence. It whispered anger when I needed clarity. It whispered urgency when I needed patience. It whispered "fix everything alone" when what I needed was to rely on the extraordinary people around me, people like Chris, whose engineering mind could decode problems I would have bulldozed through, and Kate, whose intuition and steadiness often saw ten steps ahead emotionally before I even realized a storm was forming.

The internal enemy doesn't only weaponize your weaknesses. It also weaponizes your strengths. My strength has always been my fire, my willingness to run through walls, to operate at ten times the pace of most humans, to push when others coast, to demand excellence when the room would settle for good enough. But that same fire, unchecked, becomes destructive. I've always operated with intensity, but in the early stages of building LARC, intensity became the mask for fear. Fear that the past would repeat itself. Fear that if I slowed down, everything would fall apart. Fear that if I stopped moving, the world would catch up and knock me back into the ruins I'd once crawled out of.

The war with yourself isn't about extinguishing these instincts. It's about mastering them. It's about recognizing when your mind is reacting to the present and when it's reenacting the past. It's about knowing which impulses belong to the battlefield you once survived and which impulses belong to the empire you're now trying to build.

This internal war escalates as the company grows because growth exposes the parts of you that were never designed for leadership. Visionaries are often born from chaos, but leadership requires emotional architecture. Builders often rise from adversity, but leadership requires stability. Survivors often learn to trust no one, but leadership requires trust in everyone who carries the mission with you. This is the point where many founders find themselves alone not because they have no support, but because they haven't yet learned how to accept it.
I had to learn, slowly, painfully, that carrying everything alone wasn't strength. It was trauma disguised as resilience. It was independence born from necessity, not preference. It was a habit formed in the years where no one showed up for me, not a habit suited for the years where extraordinary people surrounded me. The war with yourself begins in isolation, but it's won through connection.

Breaking the Old Patterns

Every founder reaches a moment where the company starts demanding a more evolved version of them, not in skills, but in psychology.

You begin to see your own patterns in the way the business moves. The places where you hesitate become the places the company slows. The places where you push too hard become the places the company fractures. The places where you avoid conflict become the places where misalignment festers. The places where you distrust become the places where communication fails. The company becomes a mirror and that mirror is merciless.

At first, this feels like exposure. Like the world's suddenly seeing your internal flaws in high definition. But eventually, you realize that the company isn't punishing you. It's teaching you. It's showing you that the next level requires the surrender of the old self. It's showing you that the walls you built for emotional safety are incompatible with a mission that requires visibility, collaboration, vulnerability, trust, and steady leadership.

For me, the biggest pattern I had to break was the instinct to use force when finesse was needed. I'd spent so many years fighting, fighting circumstances, fighting for opportunity, fighting to survive, that I'd become conditioned to see everything as a battlefield where aggression was the primary tool.

That mentality created the early breakthroughs in my life. It helped me survive what should have broken me. But LARC wasn't meant to be built with brute force. It was meant to be built with intelligence, partnership, engineering discipline, emotional steadiness, strategic clarity, and long term vision. Not a hammer. A blueprint.

Another pattern was the instinct to always expect the ground to fall out from under me. When you've lived through enough collapses, emotional, financial, relational, you develop a sixth sense for impact. You brace without realizing you're bracing. You prepare for the worst even when the best is happening. This becomes a silent sabotage. You don't allow yourself to enjoy wins. You celebrate victories less than you should. You anticipate failure even when success is unfolding. You dampen your own momentum because your nervous system still believes you're living in the past.

Breaking these patterns didn't happen in a single moment of clarity. It happened in thousands of micro adjustments. Small moments where I chose not to tighten, not to overreact, not to default to intensity, not to assume the worst. Moments where I consciously stepped into the identity of a CEO instead of the identity of a survivor. Moments where I let the team carry weight instead of sprinting ahead alone. Moments where I let Chris lead sections of the mission without trying to steer from the background. Moments where I let Kate's intuition settle my own. Leadership, in its truest form, is the art of not repeating the past.

When founders fail, it's almost always because they choose familiarity over evolution. They cling to the old emotional architecture because change feels like a threat. But refusing to evolve is the most dangerous choice of all. The company will grow. The world will shift. The stakes will heighten. And the founder must rise with it or be crushed by it.

The war with yourself is ultimately a war between the person you learned to be and the person you're meant to become. Most people never win that war because they never accept that transformation is nonnegotiable. But for founders, true founders, transformation isn't just a requirement. It's destiny.

The Internal Victory

You know you've won the war with yourself when the internal noise goes quiet. Not gone, just quiet enough that it no longer dictates your decisions. You begin to feel room inside your mind. Space. Clarity. A calmness that doesn't match the chaos of the outside world, which confuses everyone around you until they realize that nothing external has changed, you have.

You begin to recognize doubt without obeying it. You begin to recognize fear without submitting to it. You begin to recognize anger without weaponizing it. You begin to recognize old patterns without reenacting them. You begin to recognize the old self's voice as something separate, something historical, something no longer suited to lead. This is when the business changes. Culture strengthens. Leadership sharpens.

Decision making accelerates. The team feels the shift. The mission feels unshakeable. The entire organization stops reacting and starts executing. Internal victory isn't the absence of the old self. It's mastery over it. And mastery breeds momentum.

Once you've won the war with yourself, the company becomes a different creature. You stop operating from survival and begin operating from purpose. You stop reacting and begin designing. You stop bracing and begin building. You stop fearing collapse and begin engineering expansion.
This prepares you for the next truth:

Purpose isn't a slogan. Purpose is a weapon. It's not inspirational. It's structural. And it becomes the force that will carry you through the battles ahead.

"You can stand anything if you know what it is for."

- Eleanor Roosevelt

11

Purpose as a Weapon

When Purpose Stops Being a Slogan

Purpose is one of the most misused words in entrepreneurship. People treat it like branding, like language for a pitch deck, like something you add to a website to look meaningful. But purpose, in its real form, is neither poetic nor marketable. It's not soft. It's not decorative. It's not a mission statement typed onto a wall.

Purpose is structural. Purpose is the spine. Purpose is the thing that remains standing when everything else falls apart. Purpose is what you hold when you have nothing left to hold. Purpose is the weapon that cuts through the fog of uncertainty when the world goes dark.

And it becomes essential the moment you realize that external motivation will never be enough to carry you through the wars ahead.

The early stages of entrepreneurship are fueled by excitement, vision, adrenaline, and the intoxicating belief that you can change something. But excitement fades. Vision blurs. Adrenaline drains. Belief trembles under the weight of setbacks. Every founder eventually reaches the moment when the narrative grows quiet and the grind becomes deafening. Purpose is the only force that continues moving when everything else stops.

For me, purpose didn't arrive as inspiration. It arrived as necessity. After the losses, the betrayals, the emptiness, the rebuild, the resurrection, purpose became the thing I clung to in order to stay alive in the mission. It wasn't abstract. It was visceral. It was something I could feel in my bones. I knew that if I didn't build LARC, if I didn't create something that justified the pain I'd lived through, then the suffering would have no meaning. And human beings can endure enormous suffering if they know it leads somewhere, but they crumble under suffering that feels pointless.

Purpose gave my suffering direction. It turned my past into kindling. It turned my scars into strategy. It turned my fire into discipline. It transformed rage into precision. And it created an internal posture that nothing external could override. Purpose isn't merely what you build. Purpose is who you become while building.

It transforms you from someone who wants success into someone who requires meaningful impact. It forces you to stop measuring your life in accolades and start measuring it in alignment. It demands that you stop chasing validation and instead chase inevitability. Purpose makes you dangerous not because you're fearless, but because you're anchored. You're no longer moved by shallow incentives. You're moved by something deeper, something immovable. This is why purpose becomes a weapon. Not a shield. Not a banner. A weapon.

Because the world will push against you. Markets will push against you. Doubt will push against you. People you trusted will push against you. Circumstance will push against you. And the only thing that can push back with equal force is the conviction that your work isn't optional. Purpose is the thing that refuses to let you quit.

The Shift From Want to Must

There's a moment in every founder's journey when the mission shifts from something they want to something they must pursue. It's the moment the work stops being optional. It's the moment you realize that your life, your calling, your identity, your sense of meaning have all converged into a single direction, and that turning back is no longer possible.

This shift isn't romantic. It's not inspirational. It's not accompanied by clarity or comfort. It's accompanied by pressure. It's accompanied by fear. It's accompanied by an overwhelming sense that if you don't rise into the next version of yourself, the mission will die in your hands. Purpose doesn't whisper. It demands.

In the years when LARC was still emerging, when the world hadn't yet understood the scale of the transformation we were building, I felt this shift. It was the moment the company stopped being an idea and became a responsibility. I looked at the industries we served, cloud, AI, hyper scale, aerospace, robotics, and realized that the world's most important technologies were being transported in something that belonged in a museum. I saw the inefficiency, the waste, the fragility, the environmental destruction, the billions of dollars lost every year because no one had been willing to rebuild the system from the ground up. At that point, purpose took me by the throat.

This wasn't about a company anymore. This was about building an infrastructure the world desperately needed. It was about designing the foundation for the next era of technological progress. It was about creating a platform to move the most valuable products on earth, reduced global waste, slash costs, and set a new standard for how industries should operate. Once that realization crystallized, the mission became a moral obligation. And obligation is far stronger than motivation.

When you operate from must, you no longer negotiate with yourself. You no longer lower standards to feel comfortable. You no longer wait for perfect conditions. You no longer need permission. You no longer care about the opinions of people who aren't in the arena. You no longer ask whether you're capable. You ask what must be done next. Purpose removes excuses the way fire removes oxygen. And this shift is what transforms a founder from a dreamer into a force.

The Anatomy of a Founder's Purpose

A founder's purpose is never born from comfort. Comfort produces complacency. It produces lifestyle entrepreneurs. It produces people who want the title, the aura, the aesthetic of entrepreneurship without the price. True purpose, the kind that turns into a weapon, emerges only from people who've lived through something that carved them open.

Your purpose comes from your fracture.

It comes from the part of your life where something went wrong.
It comes from the emptiness you had to rebuild from.
It comes from the moment you realized no one was coming to save you.
It comes from the lessons you learned in silence.
It comes from the parts of your story you wouldn't repeat but wouldn't erase because they forged the core of who you are now.

For some founders, the fracture is poverty. For others, it's identity. For others, it's illness. For others, it's displacement. For others, it's a dream denied. For others, it's a wound inflicted by someone they trusted. For some, it's the constant anger of being underestimated. For others, it's the boredom of a life too small for their mind.

But the pattern's always the same: purpose comes from pain. And when you convert that pain into a mission, the mission becomes unstoppable. My purpose came from the combination of loss, betrayal, instability, reinvention, rage at inefficiency, contempt for mediocrity, a refusal to accept systems that obviously don't work, and a deep belief that human beings are capable of far more than the world encourages them to pursue. When you put all of that together, you get someone who sees broken systems and can't tolerate leaving them broken. You get someone who has no patience for excuses. You get someone whose default response to stagnation is war. I don't build because it's fun. I build because the alternative feels like spiritual death. That's purpose.

Purpose Beyond Self

Once purpose takes hold, life begins to reorganize itself around it with an almost surgical precision, as if the world recognizes the mission before anyone else does. People who once fit comfortably into your orbit begin to drift away because they're tied to a version of you that no longer exists. Others, the ones built for the next chapter, gravitate toward you almost instinctively. Opportunities sharpen or dissolve based on alignment rather than appetite. What once felt urgent becomes irrelevant, and what once felt small becomes pivotal. Purpose acts like a natural filtration system, clearing out anything that doesn't belong to the future you're building. It strips away noise, softens distractions, clarifies priorities, and leaves you with a path that feels narrower but far more powerful.

This alignment becomes vital as the inevitable dark seasons arrive. When capital dries, when a big customer hesitates, when timelines stretch, when the work becomes heavier than your shoulders feel capable of holding, purpose becomes the compass that doesn't move. You stop leading from ego and instead lead from clarity. You stop seeking validation and begin seeking progress. You stop entertaining every idea and begin entertaining only the ones that sharpen the mission. Purpose simplifies everything, but in that simplicity lies tremendous force. You're no longer trying to be everything to everyone. You're trying to become the exact person the mission requires. And that mission, in its purest form, is never just about you.

The deeper LARC grew, the more undeniable this truth became. What started as an engineering vision, to replace archaic wooden crates with a new paradigm of modular, reusable, sustainable systems, expanded into something far more important. LARC wasn't just about technology or logistics. It was about building a platform that would, by design, give back to the world. That's how HAVEN was born, from the recognition that if you're going to build something that touches global industries, that moves the world's most valuable products, that interfaces with the supply chain arteries of nearly every major continent, then you also have both the opportunity and the responsibility to use that reach for something greater than profit.

HAVEN became the moral architecture running parallel to the engineering architecture. It became a promise that LARC's growth wouldn't be one dimensional. It wouldn't be merely commercial. It wouldn't be measured only in revenue, partnerships, and scale, but also in impact. HAVEN redirected a portion of LARC's success toward fighting one of the darkest realities of our time, human and sex trafficking. It connected the operational backbone of a global logistics company with organizations on the ground doing the hardest, most invisible work imaginable. HAVEN became LARC's extension into the moral landscape, proof that purpose isn't only about what you build, but about what you contribute. This is where purpose becomes something deeper than vision. It becomes responsibility. Not the burdensome kind. The sacred kind.

Purpose forces you to see beyond the company you're building and into the lives that company can touch. It forces you to acknowledge that a mission fueled solely by personal ambition will eventually run out of steam, but a mission tied to the betterment of others becomes inexhaustible. HAVEN reminded me, and continues to remind every member of our team, that the work we do isn't just about engineering better crates, or scaling a logistics model, or transforming infrastructure. It's about leveraging every ounce of success to contribute to the fight for humanity itself. It's about using innovation to push back against darkness. It's about ensuring that our progress helps protect the vulnerable, elevates the forgotten, and strengthens the kinds of organizations that save lives quietly, relentlessly, and without applause.

Purpose at this level reshapes you. It sharpens your leadership with a sense of gravity. It forces you to grow into someone worthy of carrying something larger than a company. You begin to see your role not just as founder or CEO but as steward, of the mission, of the team, of the customers, of the community, of the values you refuse to compromise. LARC's purpose didn't just align my decisions. It aligned my identity. It gave every battle, every fight, every setback, every sleepless night a meaning far greater than personal success. When your mission touches something beyond yourself, quitting becomes impossible. You don't have the right to stop. The mission's no longer about you. It's about everyone who depends on what you're building. HAVEN crystallized that truth in a way nothing else could have. Purpose alone is powerful. Purpose fused with service becomes unstoppable. And purpose fused with service and faith becomes destiny.

Faith is the unseen engine that keeps you moving when logic falters. It's the quiet insistence that if your mission includes lifting others, you'll never be allowed to fall so far that you can't rise again. Faith turns purpose into a calling. It tells you, especially when the pressure spikes and the stakes multiply, that the mission was placed in your hands because you were built, through fire, through loss, through endurance, to carry it.

This is why purpose becomes the founder's ultimate competitive advantage. Anyone can imitate your product. Anyone can mimic your pricing, your strategy, your branding, even parts of your culture. But no one can copy your purpose, because purpose is born from fracture, from conviction, from pain, and from the parts of your story that only you lived. No competitor can reverse engineer why you wake up in the morning. No competitor can replicate your relationship to the mission. No competitor can counterfeit the meaning that drives you beyond fatigue, beyond doubt, beyond logic, beyond limits.

Purpose makes the founder nonreplicable. Service makes the mission nonnegotiable. Faith makes the future inevitable. Once purpose reaches this level, once it no longer belongs to you but to the world, you become something rare: a leader who doesn't move from desire, but from duty. And in that state, the mission becomes unstoppable.

From here, the next chapter emerges naturally, the moment when a founder and the team crosses the threshold that few ever reach.

Breaking Through.

"Victory belongs to the most persevering."

- Napoleon Bonaparte

12

Breaking Through

The Silent Turning Point

Breakthroughs don't burst into your life with celebration. They don't announce themselves with clarity or confidence. They first appear as tension, a tightening of the world around you, a sense that something's about to give even though nothing visible has changed. Outsiders love to imagine breakthrough as a single dramatic moment: a contract signed, a partnership won, a headline earned, a sudden shift that transforms everything overnight. But real breakthroughs are forged long before anyone sees them. They form under pressure, in the long stretch where effort feels wasted and momentum feels impossible. They begin at the exact point where most people stop, when the weight's at its heaviest and the progress is at its thinnest, when every force around you seems designed to break your resolve. That's where the breakthrough is born, not in triumph, but in compression, in the slow, grinding accumulation of pressure until the universe finally recalibrates and shifts its response to you.

Every founder experiences this strange moment when the world seems most against them just before it finally yields. The months leading up to it are often the most brutal. Nothing moves. Nothing clicks. Nothing gives. Every meeting feels like an uphill fight. Every introduction feels like a dead end. Every conversation feels like a repeat of the last, where you're explaining your vision to people who nod politely while silently dismissing the possibility that you're the one who will change anything. This is the psychological desert where breakthroughs incubate. Most people turn back here, assuming the silence means failure, not understanding that silence is the final compression before the shift.

LARC lived in that desert longer than most people know. We had the mission. We had the engineering. We had the field tests. We had the data. We had the conviction. But the world hadn't yet turned its head. We were building a solution that challenged a centuries old default, and systems don't abandon their habits without resistance. For months, and in truth, years, we were operating like rebels behind enemy lines. Limited capital. Shoestring infrastructure. Endless hours. Prototypes that needed fixing at midnight before a morning demo. A team running on vision instead of validation. We were boldly and audaciously asking trillion dollar industries to rethink something they considered unchangeable.

That alone can feel like an act of madness. But madness is where breakthroughs begin. What people forget is that markets don't shift all at once. They shift in whispers. The first signs were subtle. A skeptical engineer from a hyperscaler who once brushed us off suddenly lingered a bit longer during a demo. A procurement lead who'd never returned an email now sent one asking for more details. A VP who once dismissed the idea of reusable infrastructure asked a single, pointed question that told me he was beginning to see what we saw. These moments were microscopic but unmistakable. They felt like tremors beneath the floorboards. Nothing was visible yet, but something was changing. Something had started to move.

Our first true signal came at a large customer site thousands of miles from Tennessee. We'd been walking them through the structure of one of our early ALPHA systems, demonstrating fixturing, tolerances, collapse mechanics, the load path through the sidewalls, all the structural nuances most executives never bother to ask about. They ran their hands along the panels, examined the engineering with the kind of attention that told me something had shifted, then looked at us and said, "You guys are the future of crating." They didn't say it with excitement. They said it with recognition, like someone who'd finally stumbled into a room they'd been searching for without knowing it.

That moment was the first real breakthrough. Not because it changed anything externally, no contracts were signed that day, but because it confirmed that our internal reality was beginning to merge with the external one. Breakthrough always starts with recognition. And once recognition begins, momentum's no longer theoretical. It becomes inevitable.

The Shift from Invisible to Inevitable

There's a moment in every founder's journey when gravity changes direction. Before the breakthrough, everything feels like a push, pushing your vision uphill, pushing your company forward, pushing against obstacles, pushing against doubt. After the breakthrough, something subtle but powerful changes. The world begins to pull you instead of resist you. It's not dramatic. In fact, it's so quiet you might miss it if you haven't spent years learning the slightest variations in friction.

Suddenly, the emails you once fought so hard to get acknowledged now arrive unsolicited. The people who dismissed you months earlier ask if you have time to meet. The companies that once insisted on staying with legacy methods now want to test your prototypes. Doors open without knocking.

Meetings are offered without chasing. Conversations deepen without your prompting. This reversal is one of the most exhilarating and disorienting experiences in entrepreneurship. Not because it makes things easy, but because it reveals that you've crossed a psychological threshold. You're no longer convincing the world that what you're building matters. The world is beginning to convince itself.

For LARC, this shift was unmistakable. One breakthrough customer led to internal discussions at three more. One successful deployment opened the door to another region. One division's interest spread to a global team. The momentum wasn't explosive. It was geometric. Every win created another surface area for possibility. Every deployment became a case study. Every case study became an introduction. Every introduction became a wedge into a new conversation. It accumulates. It layers. It compounds. Until one day you realize you're no longer perceived as a startup asking for a chance. You're perceived as a force the industry needs to make room for.

What outsiders never understand is how much the founder changes in this stage. Breakthroughs don't just alter your company. They quiet the internal noise. They soften the old doubts. They steady the emotional turbulence that once made you question whether you were delusional or determined. You begin to grow into the person you were always building toward. The breakthrough doesn't inflate your ego. It calibrates your perception of yourself. You finally see yourself without distortion, not as someone trying to become credible, but as someone who's earned credibility through unrelenting endurance.

Momentum, Maturity and the New Arena

Breakthrough isn't a destination. It's a doorway. Once you cross it, the landscape shifts and the expectations with it. The world no longer evaluates you with skepticism. It evaluates you with seriousness. The meetings get larger. The partners get more powerful. The stakes increase. The timeline accelerates. The scrutiny intensifies. What was once a dream is now an obligation. What was once a possibility is now a responsibility. The pressure doesn't disappear after breakthrough, it evolves. And you must evolve with it.

The founder who survives the desert isn't the same founder who must now navigate the empire. Surviving obscurity requires defiance. Navigating breakthrough requires discipline. Before the breakthrough, you're fueled by hunger. After the breakthrough, you're tempered by stewardship. You realize that your decisions no longer just affect your own survival. They affect your team, your customers, your partners, and the industry that's beginning to shape itself around your presence. Breakthrough teaches you that leadership isn't about force. It's about clarity. It's about seeing farther than others can, and protecting the mission from short term temptation. It's about understanding that the world doesn't need another company chasing attention. It needs leaders willing to hold the line.

As LARC expanded, this truth became impossible to ignore. Partnerships matured. Deployments scaled. Our engineering went from prototype cycles to global infrastructure. The napkin sketch became hardware moving through some of the most complex supply chains on earth. The company that once fought for recognition was now shaping expectations for an entire sector. It was exhilarating, but it required a higher level of internal control, not emotional suppression, but emotional mastery. The founder must learn to stabilize the ship even as the waters grow deeper and the currents stronger.

The most important lesson of breakthrough is this: it doesn't make the journey easier. It makes the journey bigger. You leave behind the psychological isolation of the early years and step into a new arena where your impact is amplified, your choices carry more weight, and your presence influences systems far beyond your immediate reach. In that arena, you realize the breakthrough was never the goal. It was the gateway to the work you were always meant to do.

Breakthrough validates your vision, but legacy validates your life. Breakthrough is the world saying "we see you." Legacy is the world saying "we were changed by you." One is momentum. The other is meaning. And the founder who understands the difference becomes unstoppable.

Which is why the work ahead's no longer about fighting for recognition. It's about building beyond yourself. It's about transforming industries, shaping futures, elevating others, and designing a company that outlasts you.

Breakthrough is the moment your vision becomes real.

Legacy is the moment your vision becomes inevitable.

"The meaning of life is to find your gift.
The purpose is to give it away."

- Pablo Picasso

13

Legacy: Building Beyond Yourself

The Shift From Survival to Stewardship

There comes a moment in every founder's life when the work stops being about survival. In the early seasons, everything's driven by necessity, staying afloat, staying alive, proving the idea, proving yourself. The energy is intense, personal, and primal. You build because you must. You grind because the alternative is collapse. You push because there's no one else who can carry the dream across the threshold. But eventually, if you survive the long years of obscurity and pressure, something changes. The mission begins to reach beyond you. The company no longer feels like a lifeboat. It becomes infrastructure. The decisions stop being about "How do I build a future for myself?" and become "How do I build something that outlives me?" This shift is disorienting, because at first you don't trust it. You've spent so long battling scarcity, scarcity of resources, of support, of validation, that abundance feels like a trap. You keep waiting for the floor to cave in. You keep waiting for the moment you'll be forced to return to the trenches you fought your way out of. But slowly, almost imperceptibly, you realize the center of gravity has moved. People now depend on what you've built. Customers rely on your systems. Partners structure their operations around your reliability. Your team shapes their futures through the culture you've created. Legacy begins not when you feel ready for it, but when your work begins to matter to people you've never met.

This is where leadership changes form. You stop building for validation and start building for impact. You stop making choices based on fear and start making them based on stewardship. You stop fighting to prove the world wrong and start fighting to build the world that should exist. The mission no longer serves you. You serve the mission. Legacy is the moment when the mission becomes larger than your ego, larger than your insecurities, larger than the ghosts that once dictated your limitations. It's the moment when the company becomes a structure others can stand on. That's the quiet power of reaching the far side of entrepreneurship, it shifts from conquest to contribution.

Becoming the Person Your Younger Self Needed

Legacy isn't about money or recognition or scale. Those things are byproducts, not outcomes. Legacy is about becoming the kind of person your younger self desperately needed but didn't have. When you've survived the painful chapters, the instability, the doubt, the teachers who underestimated you, the environments that tried to confine you, the people who tried to diminish you, something remarkable happens. You begin to understand how many others are still trapped where you once were. You begin to see versions of your younger self in the people who join your team, in the customers who take a chance on you, in the young founders who reach out for guidance, in the partners who believe in your vision even before it's proven. You recognize the same hunger, the same fear, the same fire.

That recognition unlocks responsibility. You begin to lead differently. You become intentional in ways you weren't before. You speak truth more directly, because you remember how desperately you once needed it. You protect people from the pitfalls you fell into. You teach them how to navigate the psychological terrain you had to figure out alone. You become the person who says "I believe in you," because you know how much damage is done by the silence of those who refuse to say it. You start putting your scar tissue to work, using the lessons, the losses, the fire, and even the pain as tools to help others navigate their own evolution.

This is why founders who claw their way through the dark often become exceptional leaders. They lead from understanding, not theory. They lead from empathy, not obligation. They lead with clarity, because they remember what confusion felt like. They lead with steadiness, because they remember the weight of instability. Legacy begins the moment you decide that the next generation won't suffer what you did simply because no one stepped in to guide them.

LARC as a Living Proof of Purpose

Part of legacy is creating something that stands independently of you, a structure that carries the mission forward. LARC became that for me long before I realized it. What began as a napkin sketch in a restaurant grew into an engine of change, transforming not just an industry's outdated systems, but the lives and opportunities of the people inside it. Our work became more than engineering. It became a philosophy, the belief that progress must be built with intention, sustainability, and a refusal to accept obsolete norms. Packaging as a Service was never just a business model. It was a rebellion against waste, inefficiency, and institutional stagnation. It was proof that better systems don't emerge from waiting. They emerge from building.

But legacy extends far beyond technology and logistics. It extends into the moral architecture of a company, who it chooses to protect, who it chooses to uplift, who it chooses to fight for. That's why HAVEN exists. It's the clearest expression that LARC isn't simply a commercial enterprise, but a vehicle for impact. HAVEN channels a portion of everything we build into the fight against human trafficking, a global crisis that preys on the vulnerable, the unseen, the unprotected. The same instincts that shaped my mission as a founder, the impulse to protect, to rebuild, to challenge broken systems, naturally evolved into a responsibility to fight for people who can't fight for themselves. When a company becomes strong enough to lift others, that's when purpose transforms into legacy. HAVEN is the part of LARC that reaches beyond commerce and into conscience, the part that ensures our work is tied not only to innovation but to humanity. And as the company grows, that mission grows with it.

Legacy isn't what you leave behind in a bank account. It's what you leave behind in the world's bloodstream.

The Moment You Realize You're No Longer Building Alone

There's a moment, every founder eventually feels it, when you look around and realize you're no longer building a dream that exists only in your head. You see the team pushing with the same intensity you once carried alone. You see partners aligning their futures with yours. You see customers who trust you with their most valuable assets. You see investors who believe in your ability to move mountains. You see the mission expanding beyond the reach of your own hands.

This is a humbling moment, because it forces you to admit something you resisted for years: you were never meant to do this alone. The founder myth glorifies the lone warrior, the solitary genius, the one person who drags the vision across the finish line by force of will. But in reality, every legacy that lasts is built by many hands. Every lasting company is a coalition of believers. Every breakthrough is a collective act of resilience.

LARC's evolution reflects this truth. The team became the architecture of our success, the people who built systems from scratch, the partners who trusted us before the world knew our name, the customers who saw the value before the industry caught up, the family members who anchored me through every period of chaos. And at the center of that constellation was Kate, my partner in both life and mission, who steadied the storm, fueled the vision, and reminded me daily that the work mattered far beyond revenue or recognition. Legacy is not built in isolation. It is built in community. And that is when entrepreneurship becomes something greater than ambition, it becomes stewardship of the people who helped you rise.

When Vision Becomes Inheritance

The extraordinary thing about legacy is that it rarely belongs to the founder once it is fully formed. It begins to belong to the people who carry it forward. It belongs to the team who expands it. It belongs to the customers who depend on it. It belongs to the partners who trust it. It belongs to the younger generation watching it unfold. It belongs to the world that shapes itself around the impact of what you built.

Legacy is the moment your vision becomes someone else's inheritance.
This is the transition every founder must embrace, the shift from architect to guardian, from warrior to teacher, from survivor to leader. It is the moment you recognize the power of becoming the person your younger self needed and the person the next generation will build upon. Legacy is not about being remembered. Legacy is about leaving behind structures strong enough for others to stand on.

And that leads us into the final evolution.

"Do not pray for an easy life.
Pray for the strength to endure a difficult one."

- Bruce Lee

14

Becoming Militant

The Final Thesis

The militant mind isn't violent, reckless, or impulsive. It's disciplined intensity. It's the decision to wage psychological warfare against the parts of yourself that cling to smallness, fear, hesitation, and comfort. It's the mindset that refuses to bow to circumstances, refuses to accept excuses, refuses to be shaped by mediocrity. Becoming a militant mind means choosing a different operating system: relentless clarity, unshakable purpose, strategic aggression, and the unwavering commitment to build what doesn't exist. It's not a personality type. It's a discipline. A posture. A philosophy.

People often misunderstand the word militant because they associate it with chaos. But chaos is what happens when you lack control. Militancy is the opposite. It's controlled combustion. It's rage held in the right direction. It's fear weaponized as focus. It's pain converted into precision. It's the refusal to be passive in a world that rewards conformity. Becoming militant means becoming the unmovable force in your own life.

The Discipline of Unbreakability

What differentiates the founder with a militant mind from the average builder isn't intelligence, opportunity, or resources. It's psychological unbreakability. Not the absence of stress or struggle, but the resilience to walk through hell without losing your center. The militant mind doesn't crumble under pressure. It sharpens. It doesn't shrink from adversity. It studies it. It doesn't retreat from obstacles. It interrogates them until they reveal their weaknesses. The militant founder understands that the world doesn't reward good intentions or potential or talent. The world rewards those who refuse to quit.

Becoming militant requires mastery of the self. You must know your emotional triggers, your blind spots, your patterns, your ego, your wounds, and your fears with clinical precision. You must know how to navigate your own darkness without becoming consumed by it. You must build the discipline to rise every time you fall, not because falling is noble, but because rising is necessary. A militant mind is the decision that nothing will break you, even when everything in the world tries.

The Call to Arms

At the end of every entrepreneurial journey, one truth remains: no one's coming to save you. Not investors. Not partners. Not luck. Not timing. Not talent. The cavalry isn't on the horizon. You are the cavalry. You're the force that must move first, act first, believe first. You're the one who must create momentum when none exists, who must push when exhausted, who must see opportunity where others see dead ends. Becoming militant means accepting full responsibility for the life you're building, and the lives that will be shaped by your work.

This book was written for those who feel that pull, the internal pressure to build, to fight, to break patterns, to disrupt cycles, to rise above the path that was handed to them. It's for the ones who've been underestimated, overlooked, dismissed, or broken. It's for the ones who carry a story inside them that refuses to stay quiet. It's for the ones who feel the fire, even when no one else sees the smoke.

Becoming militant isn't about aggression toward the world. It's about devotion to your purpose.

The Mind That Endures All Storms

When you become militant, the storms no longer signal danger. They signal transformation. You stop fearing the hardship and start fearing complacency. You stop being intimidated by the unknown and start being energized by it. You stop negotiating with your potential. You stop making excuses. You stop waiting for permission. You stop shrinking.

Instead, you build. You rise. You push. You evolve. You create.

The militant mind is the final evolution of the entrepreneurial identity, the version of you that can survive any season, any drought, any setback, any betrayal, any doubt, any resistance. It's the mind that understands that your future is shaped by what you endure, not what you imagine. It's the mind that transforms every scar into structure, every loss into leverage, every failure into foundation. When you become militant, you stop trying to avoid the war.

You prepare to win it.

The Legacy of the Militant Mind

Legacy is built by those who refuse to break. It's built by those who choose purpose over comfort, mission over ego, discipline over chaos, construction over complacency. When you carry a militant mind, you build things that last. You build companies that stand beyond your lifetime. You build systems that change industries. You build culture that inspires generations. You build impact that outlives your name. You build a life that turns darkness into direction, struggle into strength, and pain into purpose.

The militant mind doesn't simply create entrepreneurs. It creates architects of the future.

If you've read this far, something inside you already knows this path is yours. Something inside you has been calling forward a version of yourself you've yet to fully become. Something inside you recognizes the fire, the edge, the hunger, the restlessness. Something inside you refuses the ordinary. Something inside you has survived too much to settle now.

This book was never meant to teach you how to build a product. It was meant to show you how to build yourself.

And now the question becomes simple:
Will you answer the call?

Because the world doesn't need more spectators. It needs more builders. More warriors. More misfits. More rebels. More visionaries. More people willing to burn the old systems and construct the ones worthy of the future.

Your life is the canvas. Your past is the training. Your purpose is the weapon.

Your legacy is waiting.

Now go build it.

"I will walk by faith even when I cannot see."

- 2 Corinthians 5:7

15

Real Faith, Real Love

It may seem unusual to place a chapter about God at the end of a book about entrepreneurship. Many would say the two belong in different worlds, one grounded in strategy and ambition, the other rooted in belief and surrender. But for real founders, the ones who build from the deepest parts of themselves, faith isn't separate from the journey. It's the absolute force beneath it. You can't build something greater than yourself, unless you believe in something greater than yourself. At some point the climb will become too steep, the pressure too intense, the path too dark, and the cost too high for human strength alone. Every builder eventually encounters a moment where identity, obsession, and resilience aren't enough. In those moments, you discover what you truly believe. I discovered it twice in my life, and both times it reshaped everything.

The first time was in that empty apartment, the one with nothing but carpet and silence. Months had passed with no sign of progress. I was emptied out, stripped of hope, stripped of identity, stripped of the illusions that once carried me. One evening, I went out for a run, though calling it a run doesn't describe what it was. I ran with nothing left to care about, nothing left to lose, nothing left inside me except the raw rage and instinct to move. I pushed myself far beyond anything I'd ever done. I had no reason to stop. The pain didn't matter. The exhaustion didn't matter. The distance didn't matter. It was as if I was trying to outrun my own history, trying to separate myself from the life that had broken me.

When I finally staggered back to the apartment, I collapsed against the wall, drenched in sweat, my heart pounding so violently I thought it might tear through my chest. I sat there with my shirt ripped off, gasping, trembling, defeated in every sense of the word. There was no fight left in me. No belief. No direction. No light. In that moment, I was truly at the bottom. Not the bottom people claim to feel when they're discouraged, but the bottom where there's no air and no sense of self.

And then something happened that I've never been able to explain in any human way. I heard God speak. Not metaphorically. Not as a feeling. Not as intuition. Audibly. Calmly. Clearly. He said, "You're finally where you're supposed to be. So let us begin."

I laughed out loud, not because it was funny, but because something inside me recognized the truth immediately. An overwhelming peace washed over me, deeper than anything I'd ever felt. It was as if the despair evaporated in an instant, replaced by a certainty that I wasn't alone, that there was purpose in the breaking, that everything had been stripped away so that something new could be built on clean foundation.

God hadn't abandoned me. He'd been waiting for me to stop carrying everything alone. He'd brought me to the lowest point so I could finally see the path upward. Less than a week later, I met the woman who would become my wife. The woman who would help restore me. The woman who would walk with me into the light I'd forgotten existed.

The second time God spoke to me was far more recent. My past resurfaced after decades of silence, forcing me to relive the trauma, confusion, and psychological chaos of that earlier part of my life. It came back with a vengeance, demanding to finally be processed, demanding to be confronted, demanding to be healed. I hadn't been strong enough to face it all back then, but now the pain returned with full force. In a moment of despair, I asked God the question that had weighed on me since my youth. "Why did You put me through all of this? Why did You let me endure that hell?" This time His answer came not in words, but in a vision. A vision of my wife and my family, the life we'd built together, the future stretching ahead of us.

I understood immediately. Not just my wife. My family. My children. My future. My success. Everything I'd ever built or would ever build. She was the pivot point that separated one life from another, the before from the after, the broken from the whole. Everything I survived wasn't punishment. It was preparation.

God was shaping me into the man she would need, the father my children would need, the builder my mission would require. Every wound taught me strength. Every betrayal taught me loyalty. Every loss taught me gratitude. Every dark season taught me how to carry light.

This is why faith belongs in this book. Because one of the most important decisions an entrepreneur will ever make is choosing who they take this journey with. It influences everything. It affects your purpose, your stability, your clarity, your peace, your ambition, your family, your legacy, your resilience, and the emotional landscape you build from.

Kate has been my North Star. She helped rebuild me when I had nothing left. She believed in me when I was still learning to believe in myself again. Together we built a life filled with our two incredible children, a home filled with joy and meaning, and a future grounded in faith. Without her, none of this would exist. Not the company. Not the journey. Not the man writing these words.

Why tell this story at the end of a book about entrepreneurship? Because in the end, this is why you do all of it. You do it for the people you love. You do it for the life and legacy you're building together. You do it because something greater than yourself is calling you to rise, to evolve, to become the version of yourself capable of fulfilling the path laid before you.

Entrepreneurship, at its highest level, isn't about achievement.

It's about purpose.
It's about identity.
It's about answering the call inside you.
It's about the people in your life so you never have to walk that path alone.

At the end of every great journey, there is faith.
At the end of every great climb, there is purpose.
At the end of every great story, there is love.

And that's where the final chapter ends.

"There is nothing noble in being superior to your fellow man.
True nobility is being superior to your former self."

- Ernest Hemingway

Epilogue

The Letter From Your Future Self

If you've made it this far, it means something inside you recognizes a truth that's always been waiting for you. The truth that you weren't born to simply survive your life. You were born to build it. You were born to shape it. You were born to become the person capable of carrying the weight of your own potential. Everything in this book has been preparing you for that realization. The collapse, the breaking, the scar tissue, the obsession, the rebirth, the faith, the purpose, the work, the vision, and the calling. None of it was random. None of it was wasted. Everything you survived is now part of the foundation that will hold the future you're moving toward.

Life won't get easier after this. In many ways, it'll get harder. But you won't meet that difficulty as the person you used to be. You'll meet it as the person you've become, and as the person you're still becoming. That's the real reward of the journey. Not the accolades. Not the recognition. Not even the success. The real reward is the evolution of your own identity. The person you get to be at the end of it.

If there's one thing I hope you take with you, it's this: you weren't meant to live a life governed by fear, limitation, or the echoes of your past. Your past was the training ground, not the final destination. Your scars were the blueprint, not the verdict. Your pain was the teacher, not the definition. You were meant to stand in the world as someone who creates rather than conforms. You were meant to leave something behind. You were meant to answer the call that's been whispering to you for years.

You know the call. Every builder hears it. It's the quiet voice that says you were made for more. The voice that refuses to fade. The voice that stays with you in the moments when everything else is silent. That voice isn't ambition. It's not ego. It's not fantasy. It's the memory of the life you were created to build.

The journey ahead will demand everything from you. It'll test your courage, your patience, your endurance, your clarity, your resilience, your humility, and your faith. But it'll give you something far greater in return. It'll give you the ability to look at the person you once were with gratitude instead of regret. It'll give you the ability to look at your scars with pride instead of shame. It'll give you the ability to look at your future with certainty instead of fear.

And at the end of all of it, when the noise settles and the world becomes quiet again, you'll understand the truth I discovered on that apartment floor, and later in that moment of revelation where God showed me a vision that would finally give me the answer I searched for.

You'll understand that you were never alone. You'll understand that God was shaping you long before you ever recognized His presence. You'll understand that every pain had purpose, every setback had direction, every collapse had meaning. You'll understand that the journey wasn't designed to punish you. It was designed to prepare you.

And when you look beside you, you'll see the people who walked the journey with you. The partner who believed in you. The children who remind you why you rise. The people who look to you for strength. The people who trust your character. The people who know your heart. These are the true rewards of the path. These are the treasures that make every sacrifice worthwhile.

In the end, entrepreneurship isn't about business. It's not about markets or strategies or deals or even the companies you build. It's about becoming the version of yourself you're intended to be. It is the proving ground. It's about answering your calling. It's about honoring the light that survived the darkest nights. It's about stepping forward with a sense of responsibility to your own potential and to the people you love.

If you remember nothing else, remember this:
Your life is bigger than your fear. Your purpose is stronger than your past. Your calling is louder than your doubt. And your future is waiting for you to claim it.

Stand up. Step forward. Begin.

The world isn't changed by the people who avoid the fire. The world is changed by the people who walk through it and emerge with truth, conviction, integrity, and faith. You are one of those people.

Now go build the life only you can build.

"The greatest gifts we receive are the people who believe in us."

- Unknown

Acknowledgements

This book, and the life behind it, couldn't have been built alone.

To my wife, Kate, whose love, strength, and unwavering belief in me have carried me through every season. You're the anchor in every storm and the reason I keep rising. To our children, Nathaniel and Samantha "Jane", who remind me daily of what truly matters. You're my purpose, my joy, and the legacy I fight to build.

To Chris Taylor, my Co-Founder , what a ride it's been so far! To his wife Lissa, thank you for putting up with the countless hours Chris and I have spent tearing things apart and building them again.

To the entire LARC Team/Family: you're the ones who take the impossible and make it real. Your grit, creativity, and belief in what we're building have transformed an idea into a movement. I'm honored to stand beside you.

To our investors and early believers, especially Brian Penzel, the first to believe. You bet on something that didn't exist, and because of that, it now does. I keep the note you gave me in my office.

To Jeff Janes, my first friend in Nashville, a better man I don't know.

And finally, to those who supported me through the darkest nights, when the path was unclear and the weight was heavy, your presence, your words, and sometimes simply your willingness to stay kept me moving forward. This book carries pieces of you in every chapter.

To all of you, thank you. This work is ours. This journey is ours. And the world we build from here will be, too.

About the Author

Sam Berman is the Founder and CEO of Logistics Advanced Research Center (LARC), a technology driven packaging and logistics company rebuilding how the world's most valuable and mission critical technology moves. A lifelong builder and relentless entrepreneur, Sam has spent decades dismantling outdated systems and replacing them with engineered, scalable solutions across logistics, technology, and global supply chains.

Under his leadership, LARC has emerged as one of the fastest growing reusable packaging platforms in the world, working with some of the world's largest hyper-scalers, technology leaders, and industrial organizations. His work sits at the intersection of innovation, execution, and defiance of legacy thinking, challenging assumptions that have gone unexamined for thousands of years.

Militant Mind: The Psychology of Building What Doesn't Exist was born from this journey. It's not a motivational manifesto, but a psychological field manual for founders, builders, and operators who choose to create what doesn't yet exist. Known for his obsessive drive, creative intensity, and refusal to accept inherited limitations, Sam continues to build "Beyond the Box", turning conviction into companies and ideas into infrastructure.

LARC
LARC

About LARC

LARC is a Tennessee born engineering and logistics technology company transforming how high value technology moves around the world. Designed for AI, Cloud, Semiconductor, Aerospace, Defense, Robotics, and Medical Tech, LARC's reusable modular CRATE systems replace outdated single use packaging with precision engineered protection, security, visibility, and circular efficiency.

Trusted by the world's largest OEMs, hyper-scalers and manufacturers, LARC delivers Packaging as a Service through a global network of partners, integrated tracking, and industry leading innovation. Driven by a mission to build "Beyond the Box," LARC is redefining sustainability, security, and performance for the next generation of global technology movement.

www.larc.co

"Blessed is he who has found his work;
let him ask no other blessedness."

- Thomas Carlyle

Bonus Chapter

Practical Warfare

Even though this book is fundamentally about the psychology of what it takes to build something meaningful, about the internal architecture that must be constructed before the external empire, I'd be remiss not to share the practical realities that separate those who merely dream from those who actually build. What follows comes from my world as an entrepreneur, from the years spent building companies from nothing, but also from my time working inside large enterprise organizations. I've seen both sides. I've worked in the corporate machine and I've built outside of it. And while the environments are different, the principles of execution, of discipline, of relentless forward motion, remain the same. Because here's the truth that no one wants to hear: the psychology alone won't save you. The mindset, the resilience, the obsession, these are necessary but insufficient.

You must also be willing to execute at a level that most people can't fathom, can't sustain, and won't attempt. This chapter isn't about inspiration. It's about implementation. It's about the unglamorous, brutal, relentless work that happens between the moment you decide to build and the moment the world recognizes what you've created. It's about the gap between intention and impact, and how that gap is closed not with vision boards or affirmations, but with massive, sustained, intelligent action.

The Mythology of Balance

Let me destroy a myth that will kill your dreams before they ever leave the ground: the myth of balance. You've been sold a lie by people who've never built anything significant. They tell you that success comes from harmony, from work life balance, from taking care of yourself first, from setting boundaries, from protecting your energy. And while these things have their place in a stable, mature life, they have no place in the beginning of your entrepreneurial journey.

In the early years, there's no balance. There's only obsession and everything else. There's only the work and the people who don't understand why you're doing the work. You'll miss things. You'll skip vacations. You'll say no to social events that once seemed important. You'll become, for a season, unavailable to nearly everyone except the mission. This is the cost of admission.

I'm not advocating for recklessness or destruction of yourself. I'm telling you that building something from nothing requires a level of focus and intensity that comfortable people will call unhealthy, extreme, unbalanced. Let them call it whatever they want. They're not building what you're building. They don't have the fire you have burning inside. Their opinions are irrelevant.

When LARC was born, when it was nothing more than a sketch on a napkin and a stubborn conviction that there had to be a better way, I didn't have the luxury of balance. I had a choice: protect my comfort or pursue my calling. I chose the calling. And for years, that calling consumed me. Early mornings. Late nights. Weekends. Holidays. Every spare moment was either spent working on the business or thinking about how to work on the business better. Was it sustainable forever? No. But it was necessary then. And if you want to build something that matters, it'll be necessary for you too.

The Doctrine of Massive Action

Massive action isn't about working harder. It's about working at a volume and velocity that creates its own momentum. It's about understanding that in the early stages of building, activity itself becomes an asset. You don't yet know what will work. You don't yet have the market feedback to know where to focus. So you do, test and try everything. You move so fast and in so many directions that something, eventually, has to break through.

Most entrepreneurs fail not because they executed the wrong strategy, but because they didn't execute enough of anything. They had one conversation with a potential customer and decided the market wasn't ready. They posted on social media for two weeks and concluded that content marketing doesn't work. They sent ten emails and determined that cold outreach was dead. This isn't entrepreneurship. This is dabbling. And dabbling doesn't build companies.

Massive action means that when you decide to pursue a channel, you pursue it relentlessly. If you're going to cold email, you send five hundred emails, not fifty. If you're going to create content, you publish every single day for six months, not twice a week for a month. If you're going to attend networking events, you go to three per week, not three per quarter. You saturate the channel. You overwhelm the opportunity. You create so much activity that the law of averages has no choice but to work in your favor.

This isn't blind action. This is informed aggression. You're not randomly flailing. You're systematically testing hypotheses at scale. You're learning faster than your competitors because you're doing more than your competitors. And in the early days, speed of learning is the only competitive advantage that matters.

The Team You Build Is the Future You Create

You can't do this alone. I know the mythology of the solo founder, the lone genius who wills an empire into existence through sheer force of personality. It's a beautiful story. It's also a lie. Every significant company, every meaningful movement, every lasting impact has been the result of a team. Not a person. A team.

But here's what they don't tell you: building a team is harder than building a product. Because people are complicated. People have egos. People have insecurities. People have lives outside of your mission. And if you don't learn how to navigate this complexity, your team will become your greatest liability instead of your greatest asset.

The first principle of team building is this: hire for alignment before competence. Skills can be taught. Alignment can't. If someone doesn't believe in the mission, doesn't share your values, doesn't have the fire to see this through, it doesn't matter how talented they are. They'll slow you down. They'll create friction. They'll leave when things get hard. And in the early days, things always get hard.

I made this mistake more than once. I hired people who looked great on paper. Impressive resumes. Glowing references. Strong technical skills. But they didn't have the hunger. They didn't have the resilience. They didn't have the willingness to do whatever it took. And when the pressure mounted, when the stakes increased, when the easy path diverged from the right path, they chose the easy path. Every single time.

Now, I hire differently. I look for people who've been through something. People who've failed and rebuilt. People who've been underestimated and proven the doubters wrong. People who have a chip on their shoulder and something to prove. These are the people who'll run through walls for the mission. These are the people who'll stay when everyone else leaves.

Communicate with brutal honesty. Not cruelty. Honesty. Your team needs to know where they stand. They need to know what's expected. They need to know when they're winning and when they're falling short. Ambiguity is poison in a high performing team. Clarity is progression.

The Selling Imperative - Why Founders Must Sell

If you're not selling, you're not building a business. You're building a project. And projects don't change the world. Businesses do.

I meet too many founders who believe that selling is beneath them. They think that if they build a great product, customers will come. They think that if they create enough value, the market will recognize it. They think that sales is something you hire someone else to do once you have product market fit. This is delusional.

Sales isn't a department. Sales is the lifeblood of the business. And in the early days, sales is your job. Not because you're good at it. Not because you enjoy it. But because no one else can sell your vision the way you can. No one else believes in the mission the way you do. No one else has the passion, the conviction, the desperation to make this work. I wasn't a natural salesperson. I was an logistician. I was a problem solver. I was comfortable with systems and uncomfortable with people. But I learned to sell because I had no choice. And what I learned is this: selling isn't about manipulation. It's not about tricks or tactics or persuasion techniques. It's about belief. It's about understanding the problem so deeply and caring about the solution so intensely that your conviction becomes contagious.

Every single early customer of LARC came from a conversation we had. Not a sales rep. Not a marketing campaign. We talked to hundreds of people. We listened to their problems. We showed them how we could solve those problems. We addressed their objections. We followed up relentlessly.

We didn't take no for an answer because I knew that no often just means not now, or not yet, or not unless you show me why this matters.

And here's what happened: I got better. Not just at selling, but at understanding the business. Every sales conversation taught me something. Every objection revealed a weakness in the offering. Every closed deal validated an assumption. Every lost deal showed me where I needed to improve. Sales became my education. And that education became the foundation for everything that came after.

If you want to build a business, you must sell. You must have the conversations. You must hear the objections. You must face the rejection. You must close the deals. And you must do this even when it's uncomfortable, even when it's terrifying, even when you'd rather do anything else. At LARC, everyone sells.

The Speed Doctrine - Moving Faster Than Fear

Speed is a weapon. In the early stages of building, speed is your only asymmetric advantage. You don't have the brand. You don't have the capital. You don't have the team. But you do have the ability to move faster than anyone else. And if you weaponize that speed, you can outexecute competitors who have every other advantage.

This doesn't mean recklessness. This means bias toward action. This means defaulting to doing instead of deliberating. This means testing instead of theorizing. This means shipping instead of perfecting.

I've watched too many entrepreneurs lose years of their life to analysis paralysis. They want to make sure they have the perfect strategy before they launch. They want to validate every assumption before they commit. They want to de-risk every decision before they move. And while they're waiting for certainty, someone else is building. Someone else is learning. Someone else is winning.

Certainty is a luxury you can't afford. You'll never have all the information. You'll never have perfect clarity. You'll never feel completely ready. And if you wait until you do, you'll wait forever. The alternative is to move. Make the decision with the information you have. Take the action even if you're not sure it'll work. Ship the product even if it's not perfect. Have the conversation even if you don't know what to say. Apply for the opportunity even if you don't meet all the requirements. The worst that happens is you learn something. The best that happens is you break through.

Speed compounds. Every action creates feedback. Every feedback creates learning. Every learning creates improvement. And improvement, over time, creates dominance.And the fastest learner is always the person who's doing the most. Stop polishing the brass get the ship out of port.

The Resilience Requirement - When Everything Falls Apart

Everything will fall apart. Not might. Will. The deal will fall through. The product will break. The team member will quit. The investor will pass. The customer will leave. The market will shift. The strategy will fail. This isn't pessimism. This is reality.

And when it happens, when everything you built starts to crumble, you'll have a choice. You can collapse with it. You can let the failure define you. You can decide that this is proof that you were never meant to build anything. Or you can remember that collapse isn't the end. It's the clearing. It's the demolition required before reconstruction.

I've been through multiple collapses. Financial. Relational. Emotional. Spiritual. And each one felt like the end. Each one looked like proof that I'd made a catastrophic mistake. Each one whispered that I should give up, go back, settle for something safer. And each time, I chose to keep moving. Not because I was certain it'd work out. But because stopping wasn't an option.

Resilience isn't about never falling. It's about getting up every single time you fall. It's about refusing to let the collapse be permanent. It's about finding the lesson in the loss, the strength in the struggle, the opportunity in the obstacle.

When things fall apart, and they will, don't ask why this is happening to me. Ask what this is teaching me. Don't spiral into pity for yourself. Get curious about the problem. Don't retreat into isolation. Reach out to the people who've been through it. Don't abandon the mission. Recommit to it with even more intensity. The entrepreneurs who win aren't the ones who never fail. They're the ones who fail and keep building anyway.

The Final Word - Execution is Everything

This book has been about psychology. About identity. About the internal war that must be won before the external battle can even begin. And all of that is true. All of that is necessary. But it's not sufficient.

You must also execute. You must also grind. You must also build the team, close the deals, manage the money, move with speed, and survive the collapses. You must do the work that no one sees, the work that doesn't get celebrated, the work that feels impossible.

And here's the truth that I need you to understand: the work is the point. The grind isn't something to endure until you arrive. The grind is the arrival. The struggle isn't the obstacle to success. The struggle is the success.

Because the person you become in the process of building something meaningful is worth more than anything you'll ever build. The skills you develop, the resilience you forge, the confidence you earn, these are assets that no one can take from you. These are the rewards that matter.

So grind. Not because you have to. But because you get to. Because you've been given the rare and precious opportunity to pursue something larger than yourself. Because you have the fire inside that refuses to let you settle. Because you're one of the few who'd rather die trying than live wondering.

The world doesn't need more dreamers. It needs more doers. It needs more builders. It needs more people who are willing to put in the work, take the risks, endure the pain, and create something that matters.

Be one of those people.

So let us begin.